LAYNE CATHERINE
PSYCHEDELEDIGITAL ARTIST
THE TAROT COLORING BOOK

I0468888

THE MAJOR ARCANA
FIRST OF THREE VOLUMES INCLUDING THE MAJOR AND MINOR ARCANA

PSYCHEDELEDIGITAL IS THE TERM I INVENTED AFTER YEARS OF STRIVING TO DEFINE MY STYLE OF ART AND ANSWER THE OFTEN ASKED QUESTION "WHAT KIND OF ART DO YOU DO?".

THE ART THAT YOU ENJOY HERE IS THE CULMINATION OF DECADES OF WORK PERFECTING MY CRAFT, AND FOR ME, IT IS ALSO A BITTERSWEET RETURN TO THE DAYS OF UNDERGROUND NEWSPAPERS.

WHAT I HAVE CREATED IS NOT FOR THE AMATEUR COLORIST, BUT RATHER FOR THOSE LOOKING FOR SOMETHING WITH A BIT MORE SUBSTANCE AND CHALLENGE.

YOU DO NOT HAVE TO STAY BETWEEN THE LINES.

THESE IMAGES ARE GIVING US BOTH THE CHANCE TO BECOME CO-CREATORS AND AS YOU FILL THE PAGES WITH THE COLORS OF YOUR OWN CHOOSING, EXPERIMENT WITH VALUES AND SHADINGS AND CONSIDER THE LINES AS IDEAS, GUIDES, A BLUEPRINT, NOT A COMMAND... THEN YOU WILL BE WITH ME, IN THAT SPACE OF CREATIVITY THAT BRINGS EACH ARTIST INTO A HIGHER REALM.

WELCOME TO MY WORLD!

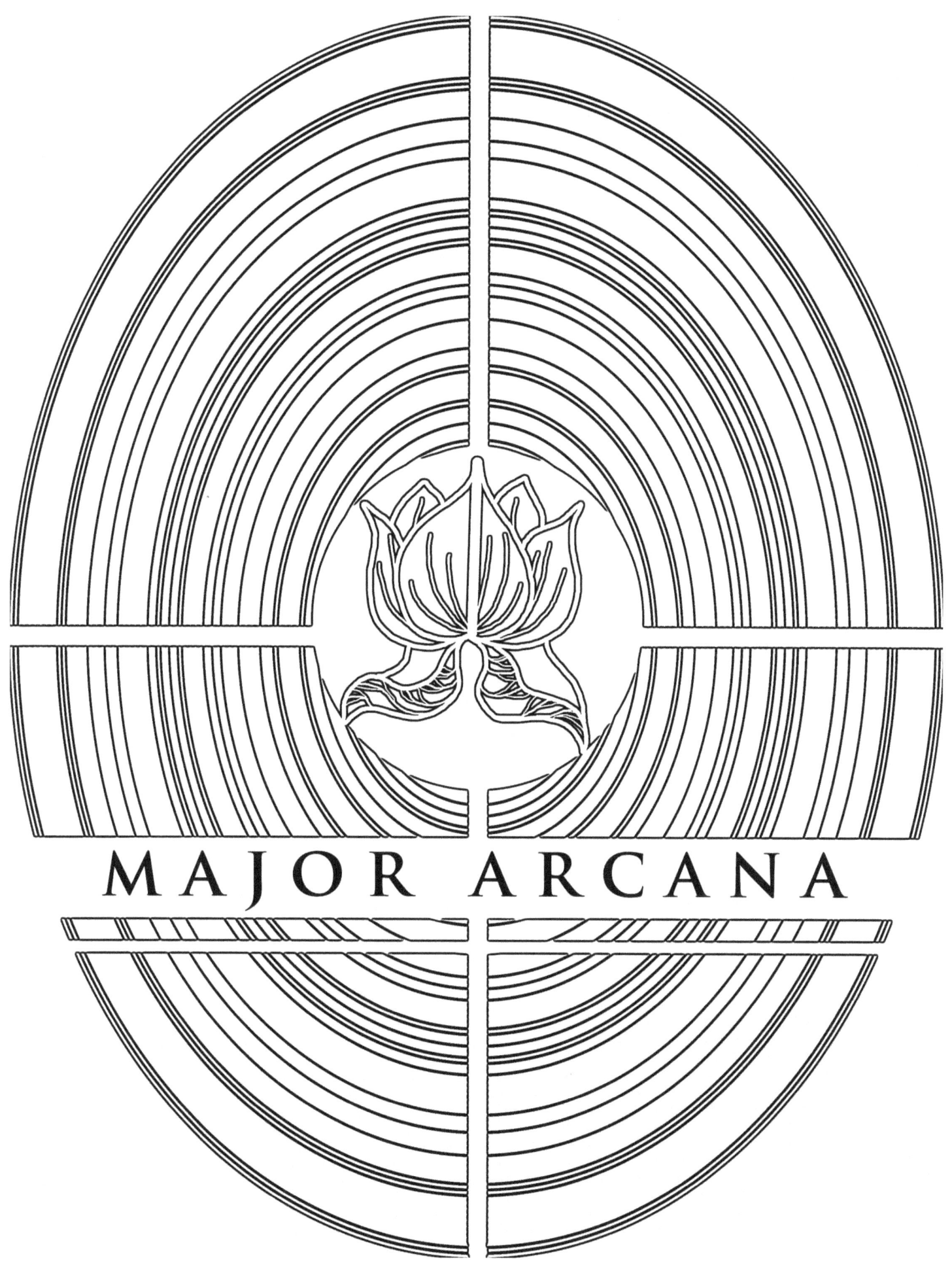

MAJOR ARCANA

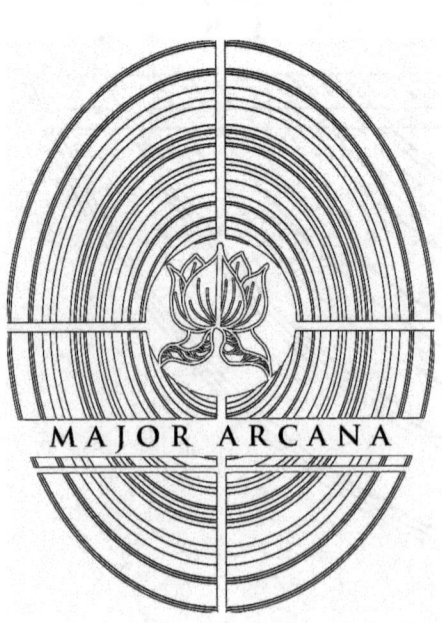

MAJOR ARCANA

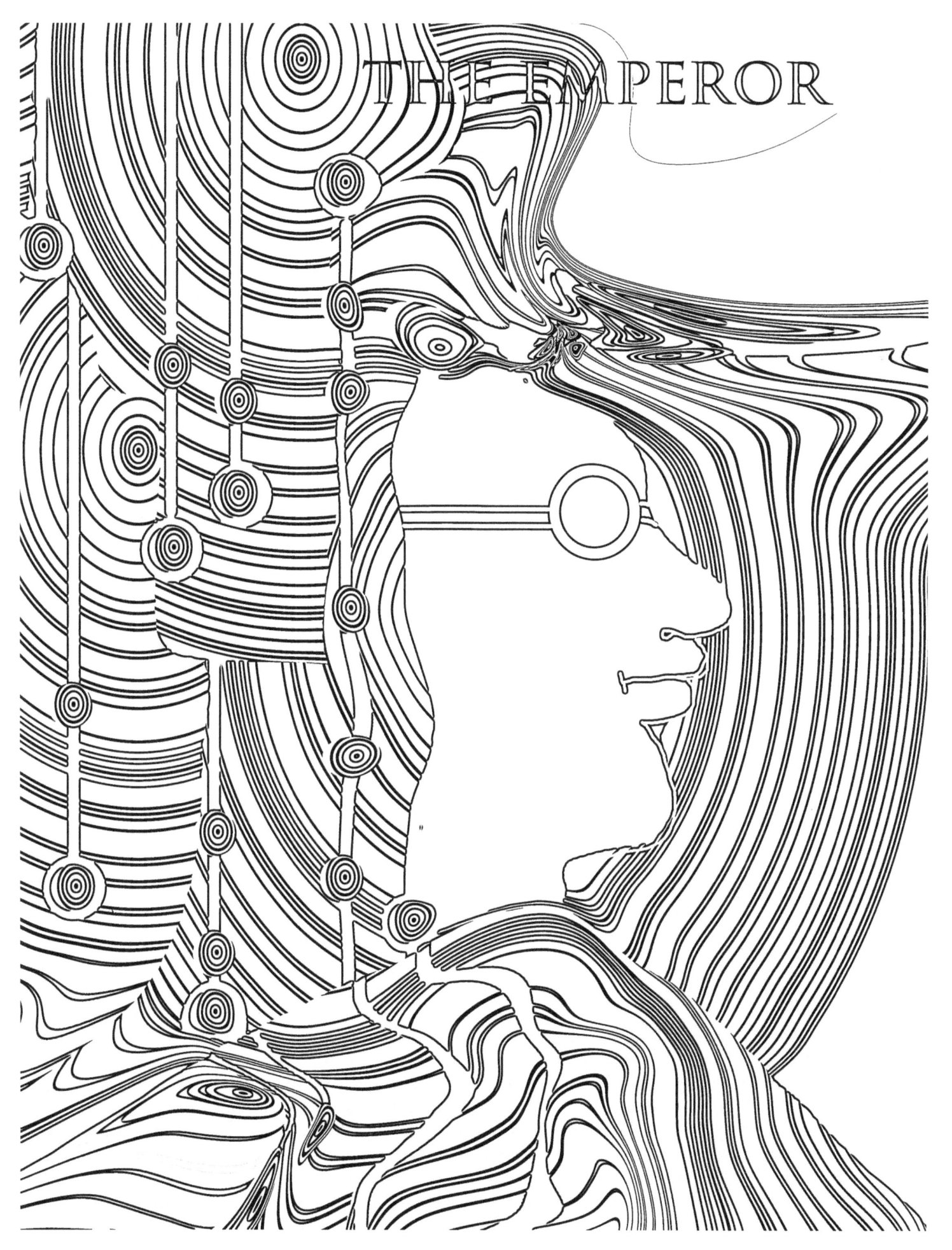

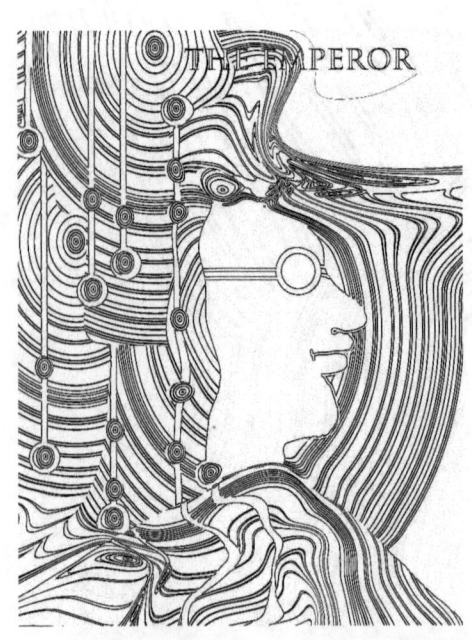

THE EMPEROR

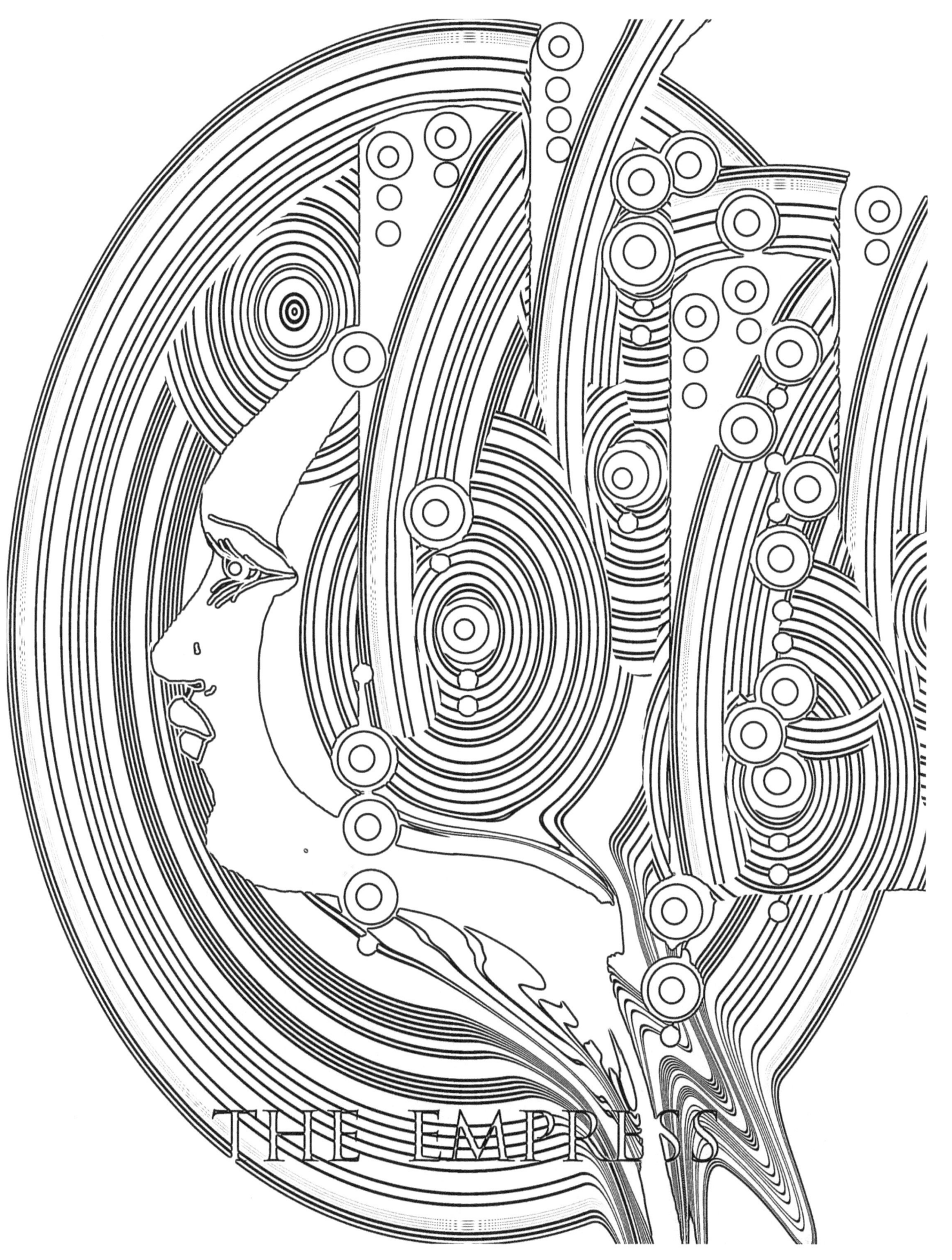

THE EMPRESS

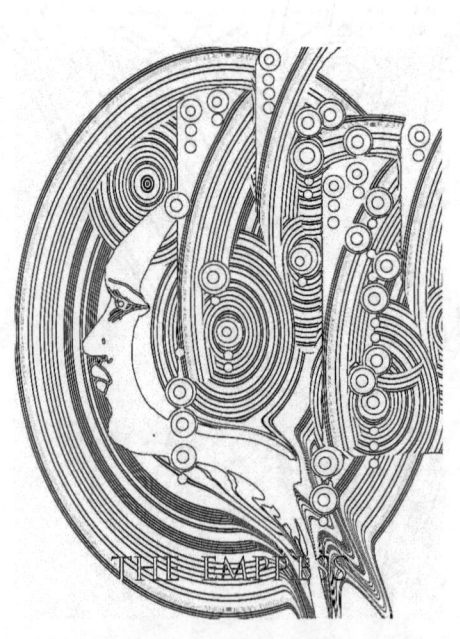

THE EMPRESS

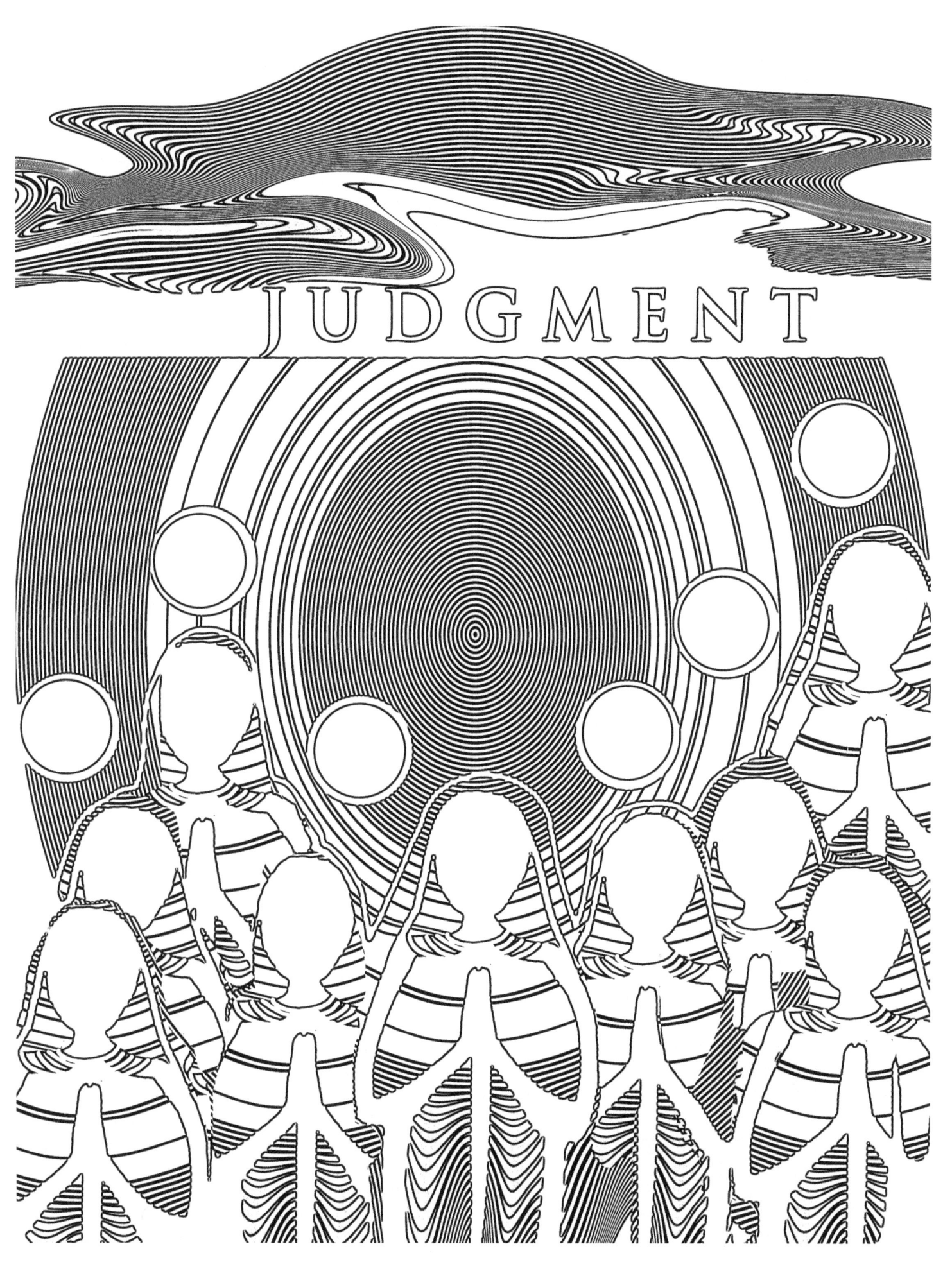

JUDGMENT

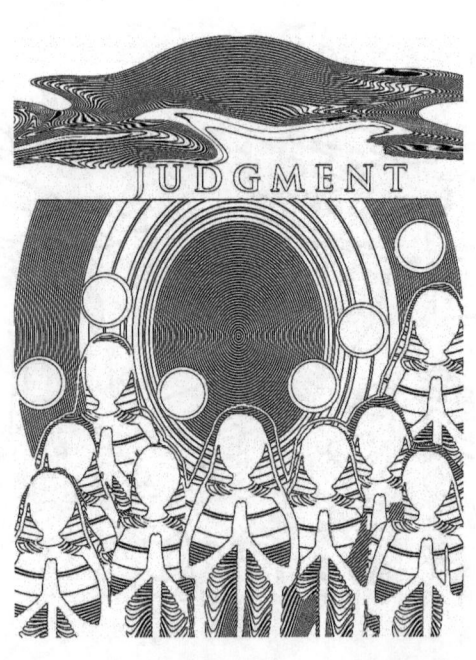

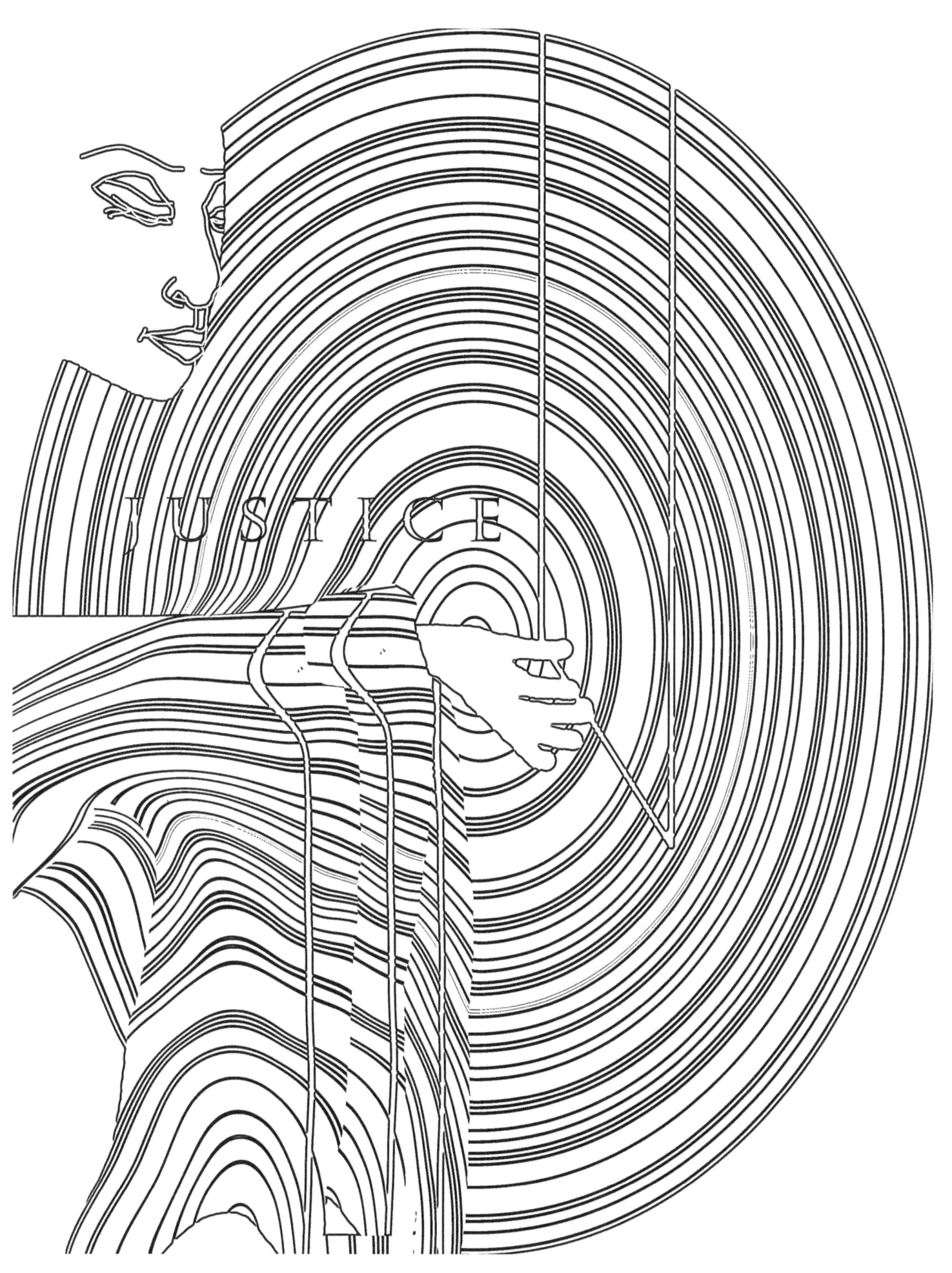

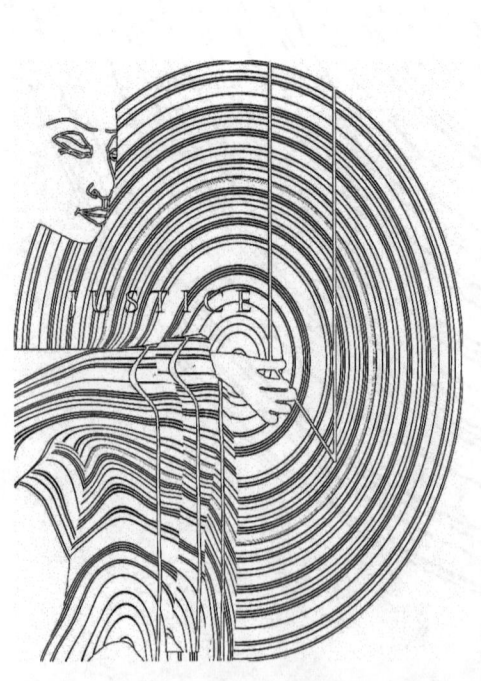

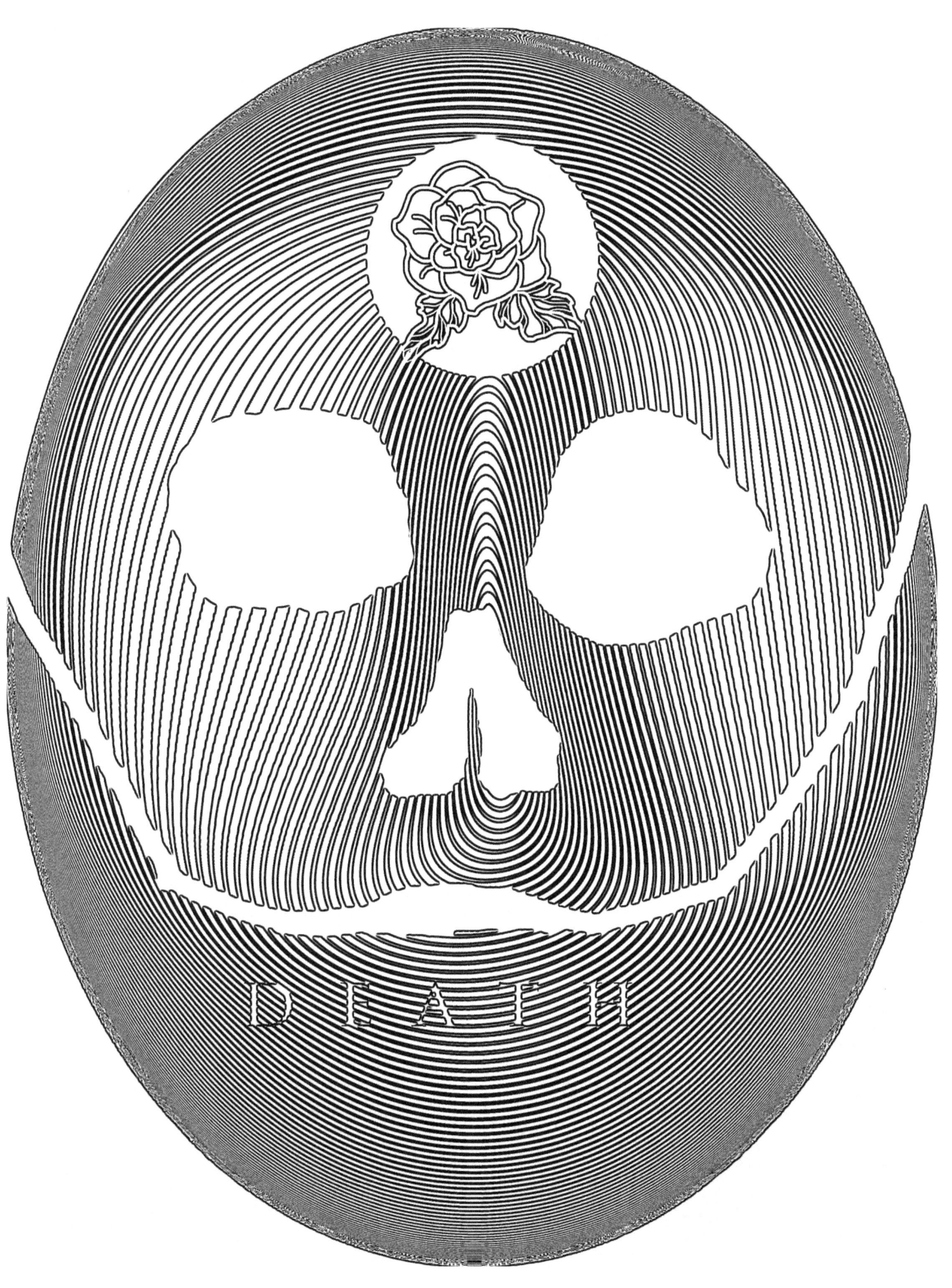

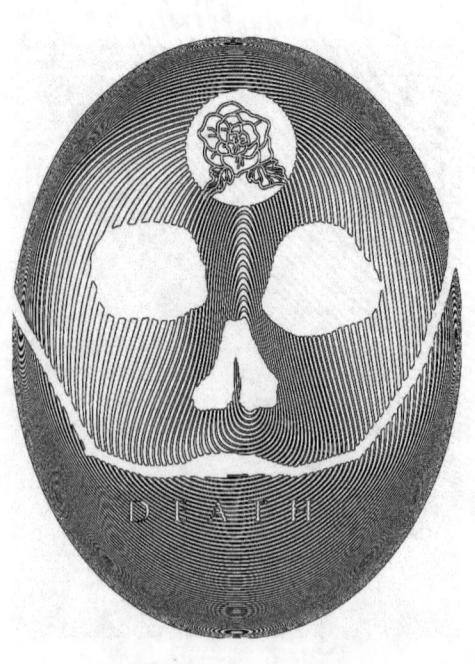

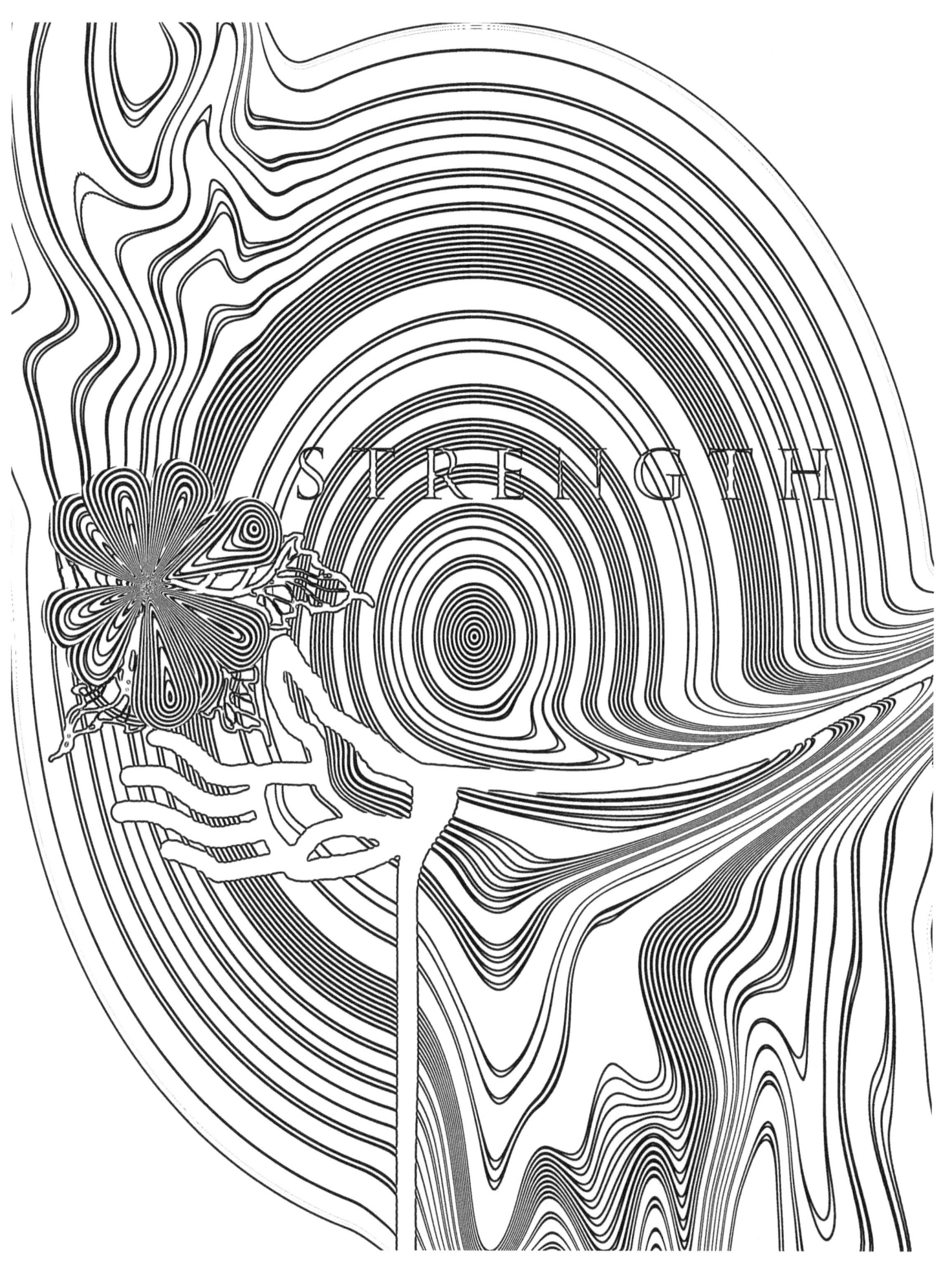

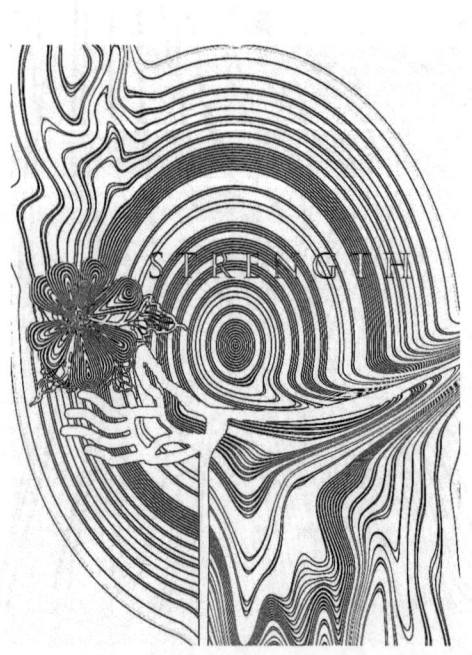

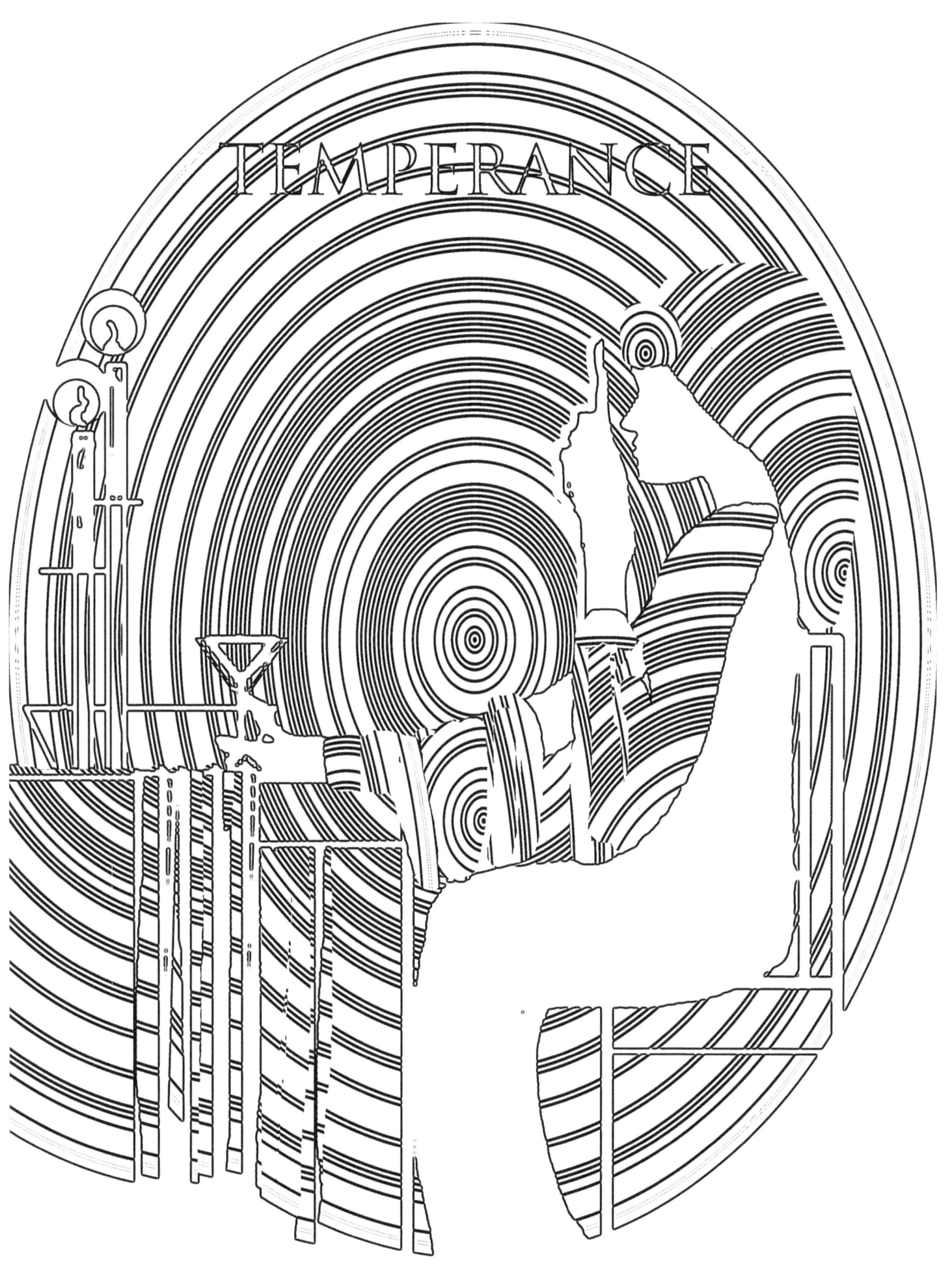

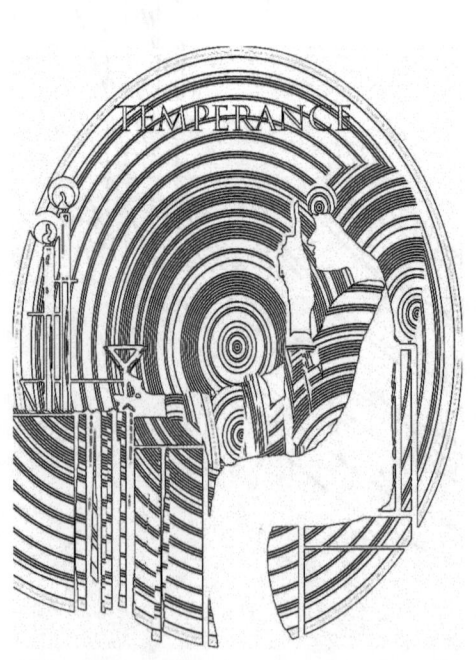

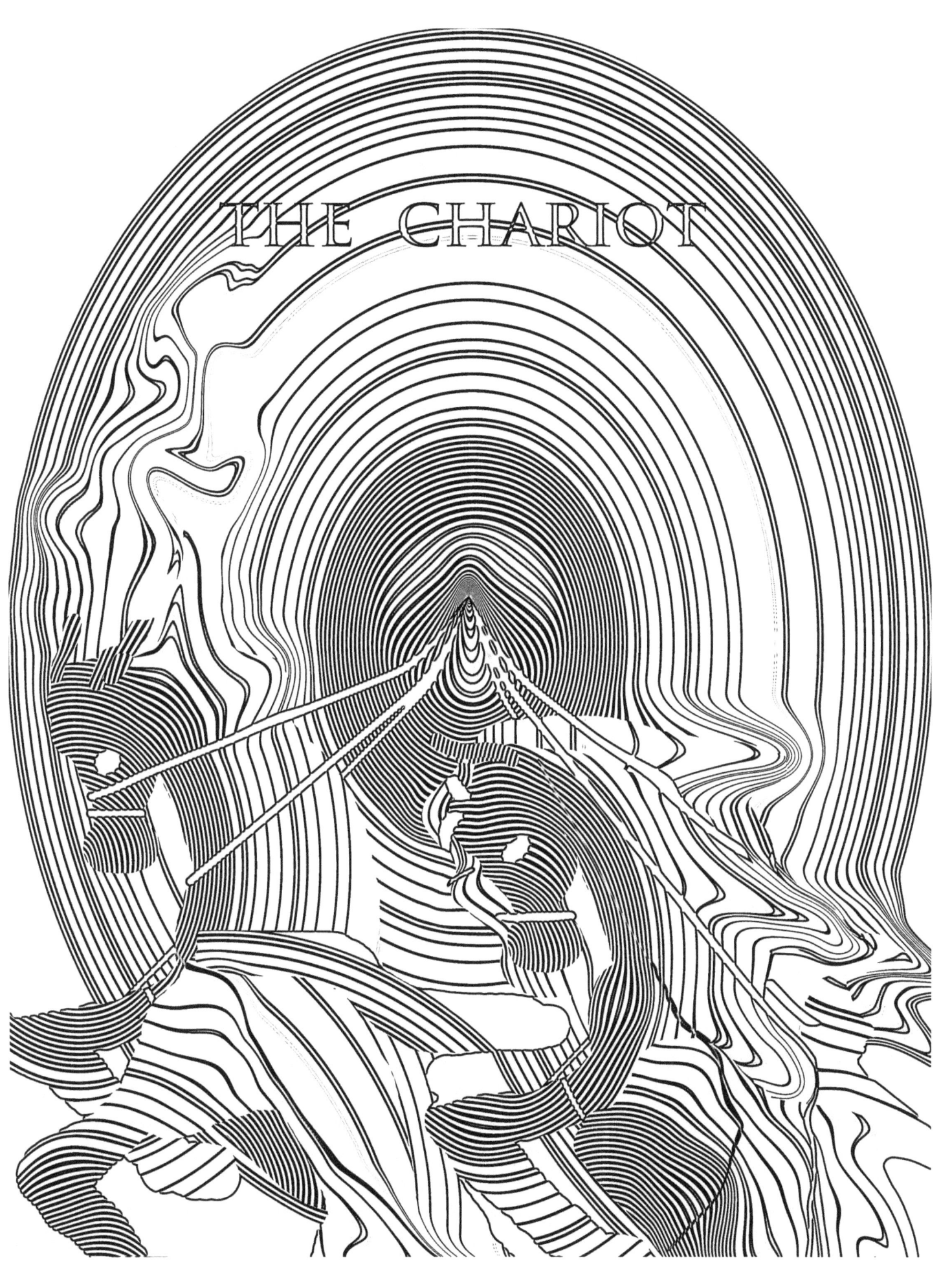

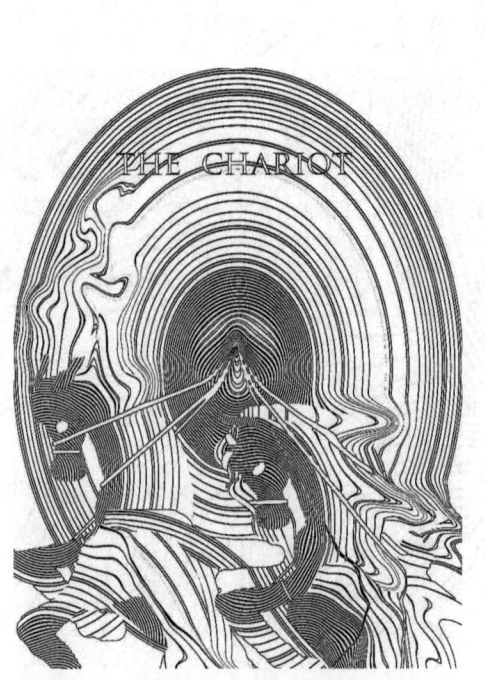

THE CHARIOT

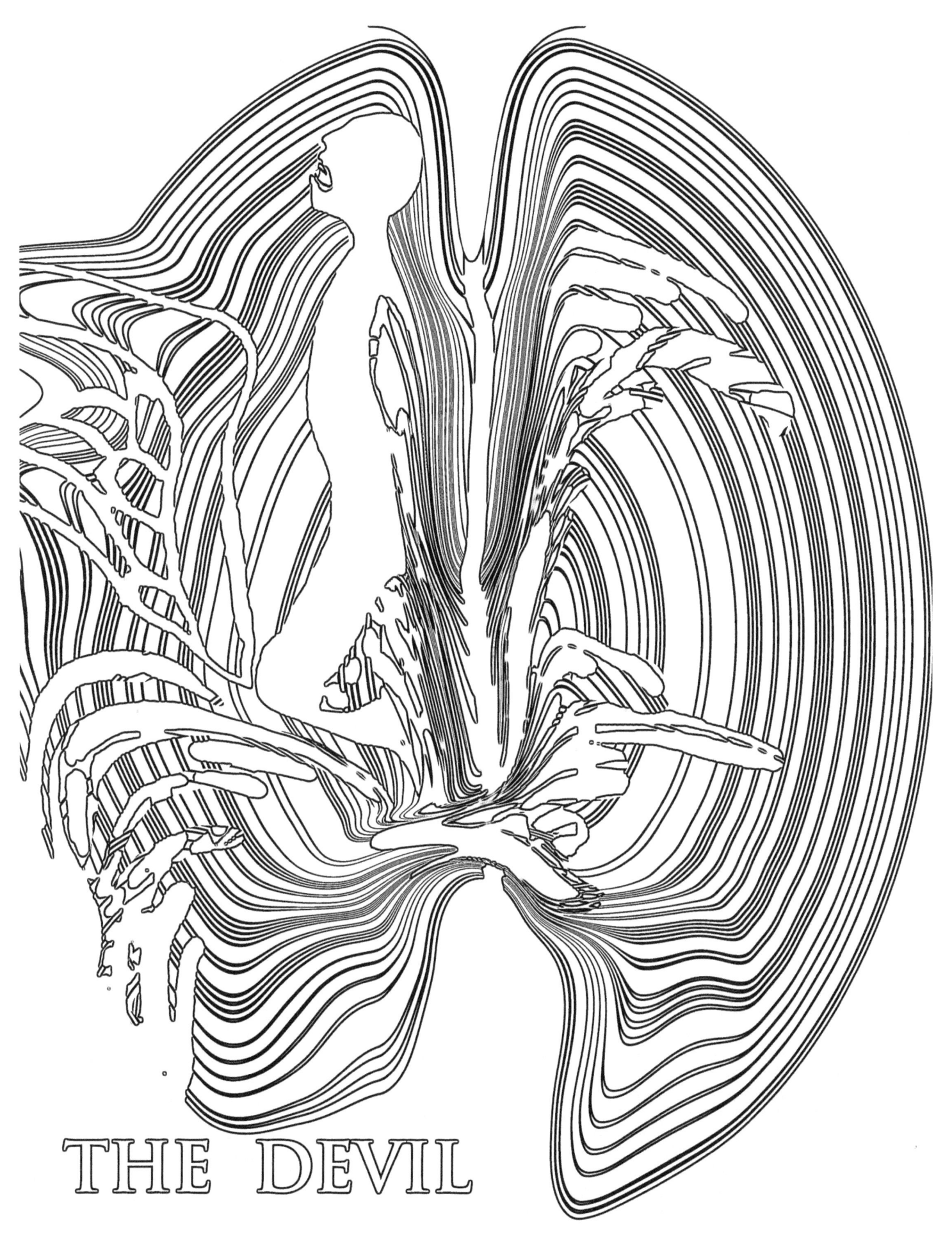

THE DEVIL

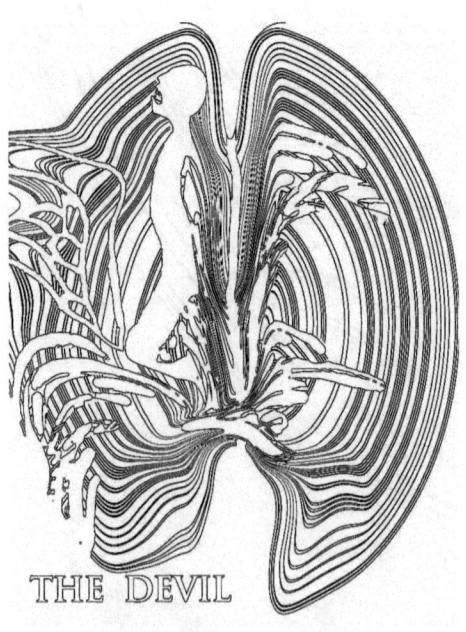

THE DEVIL

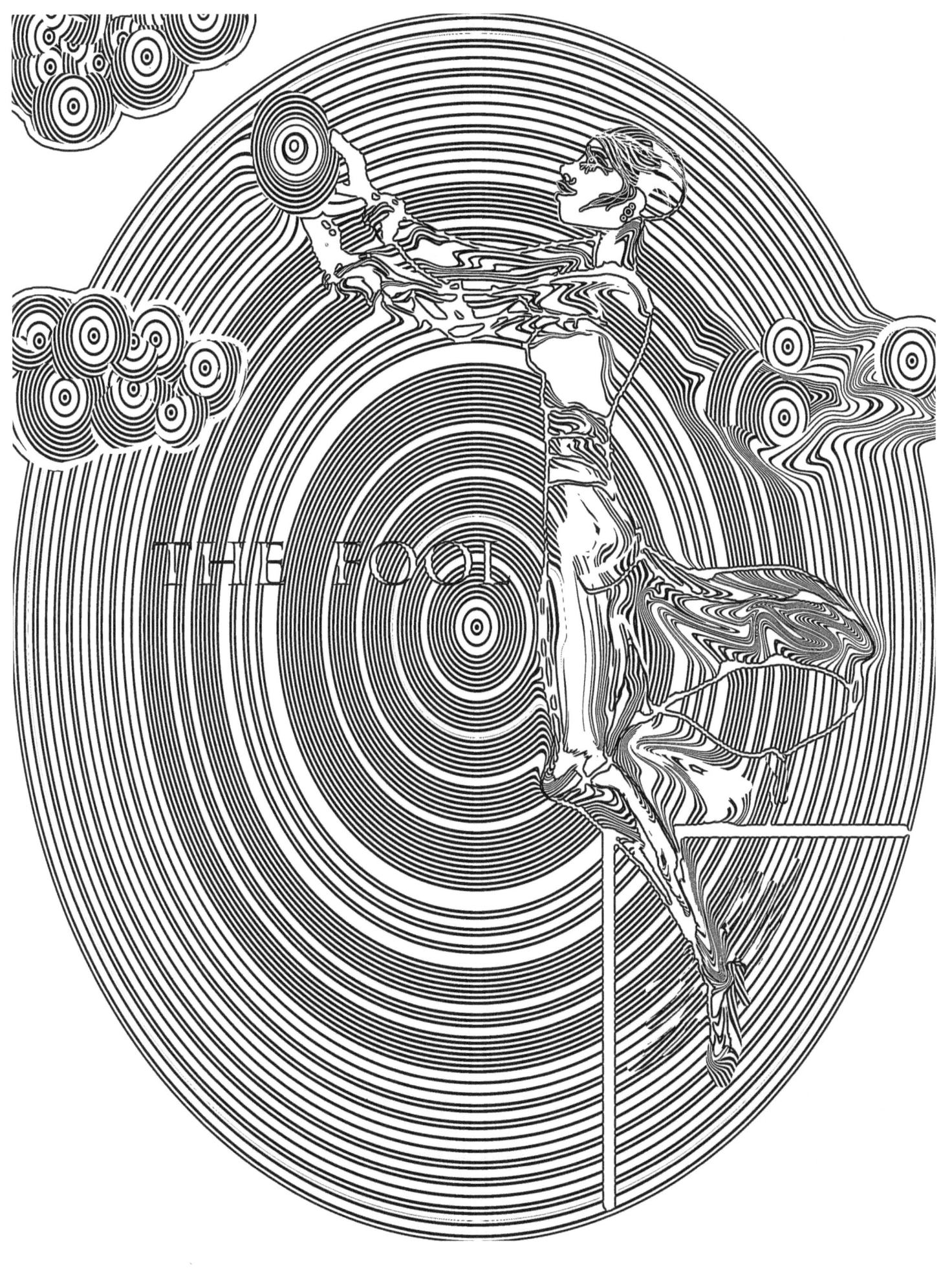

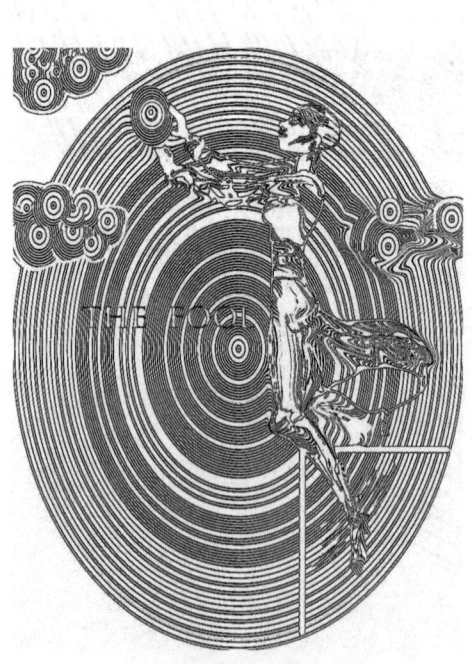

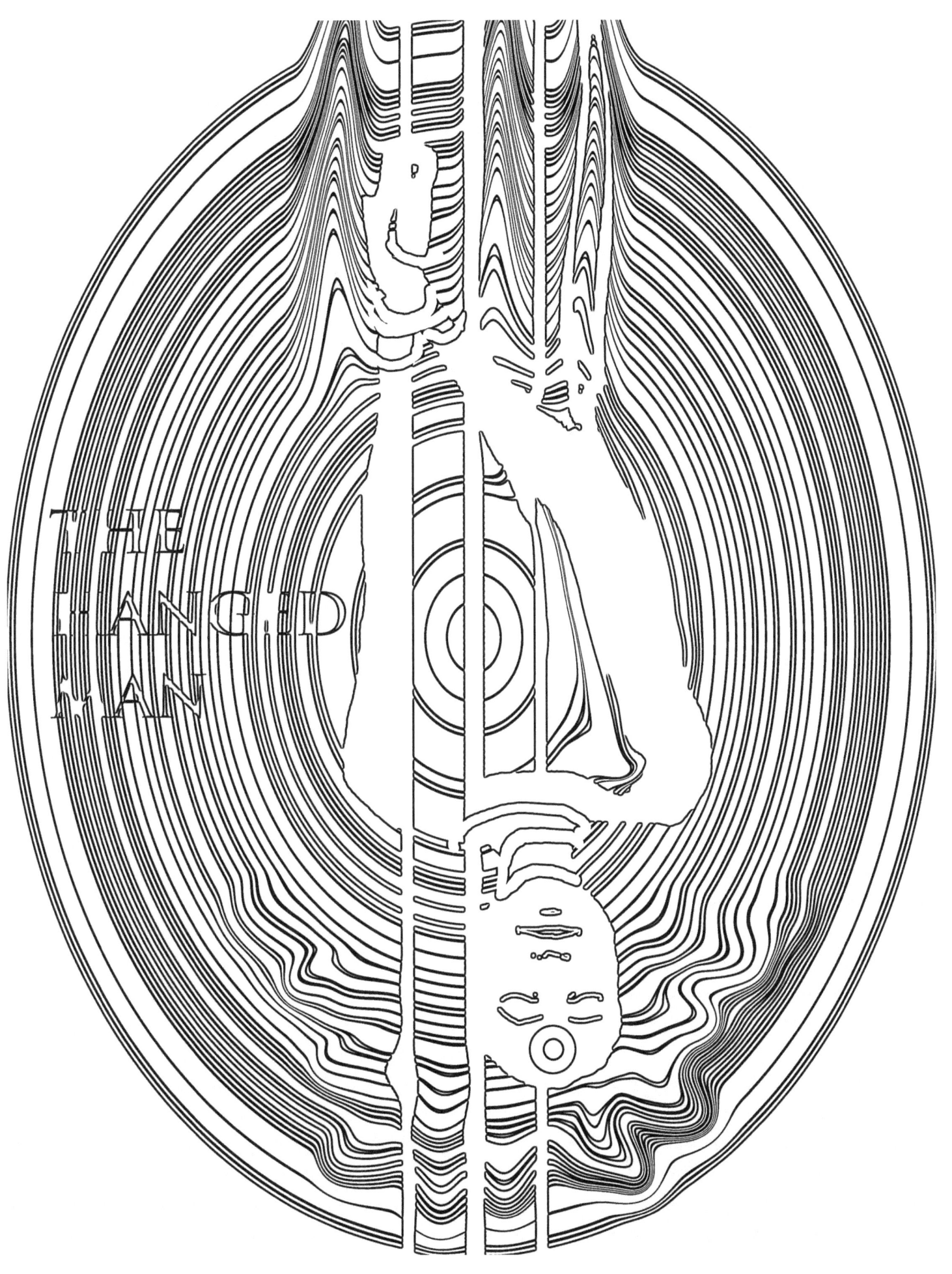

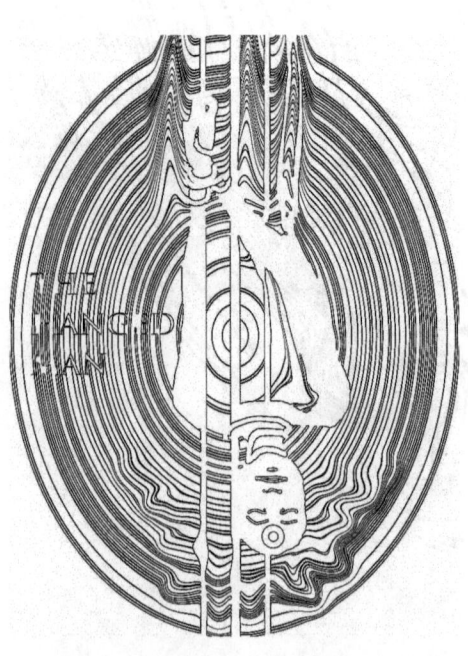

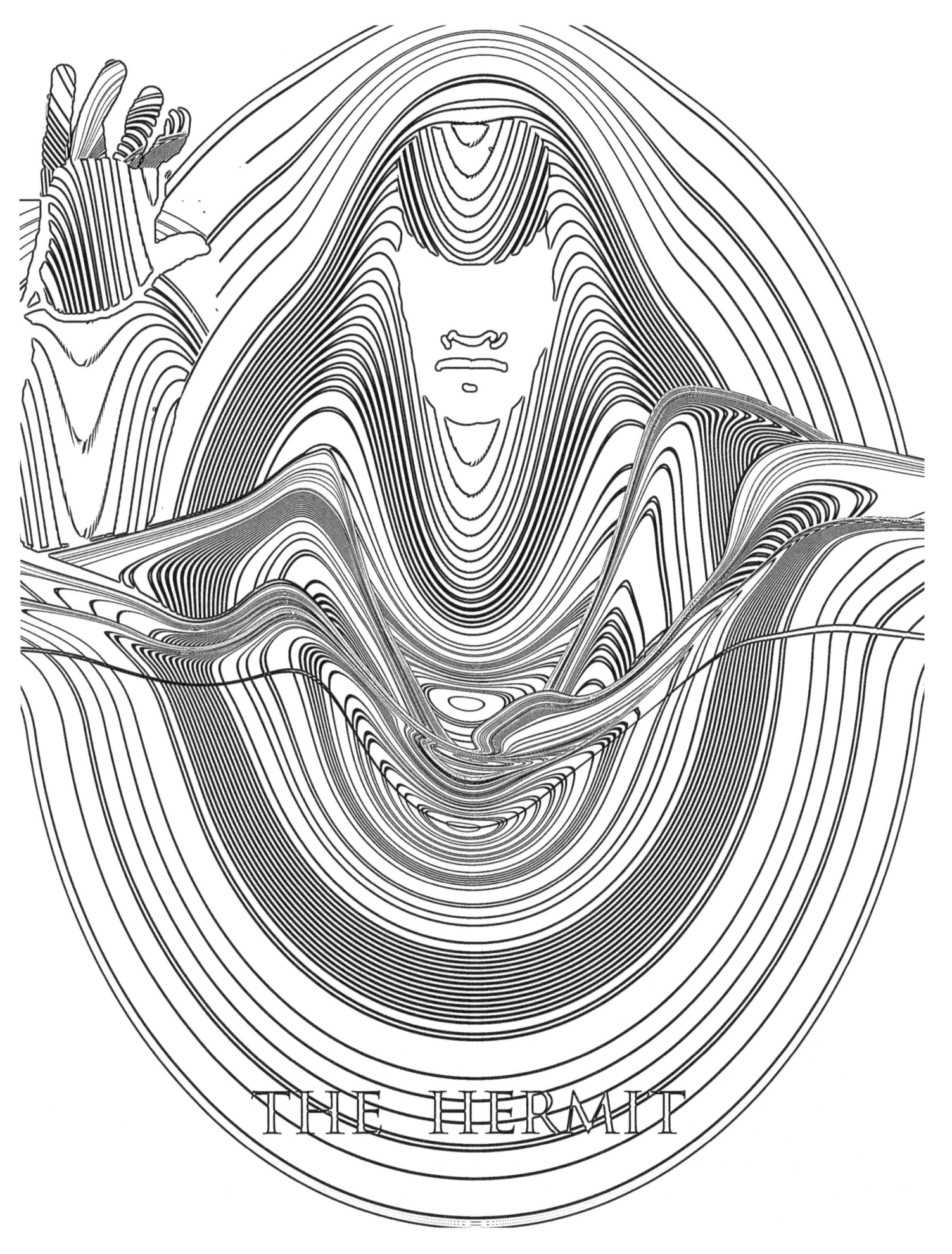

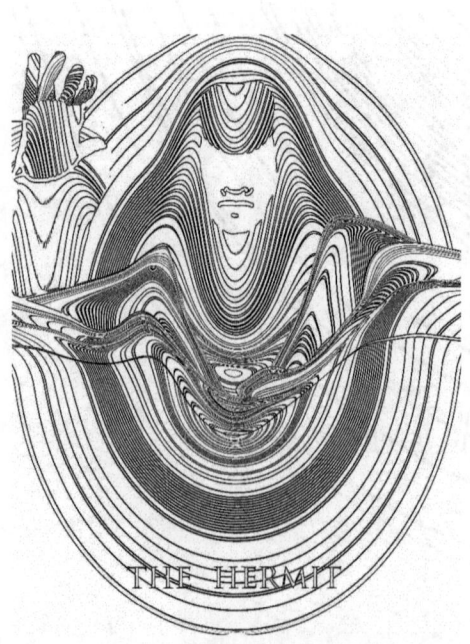

THE HERMIT

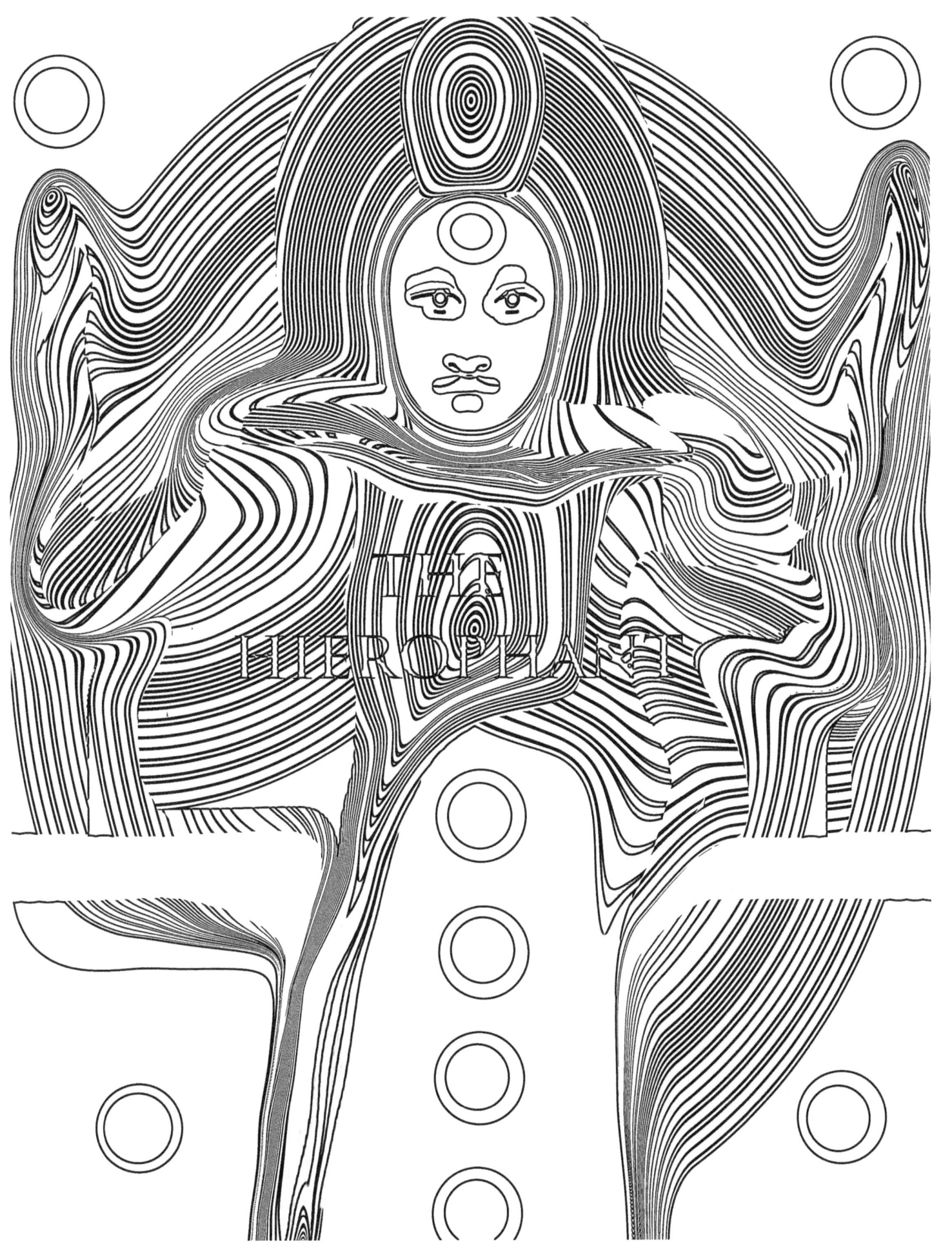

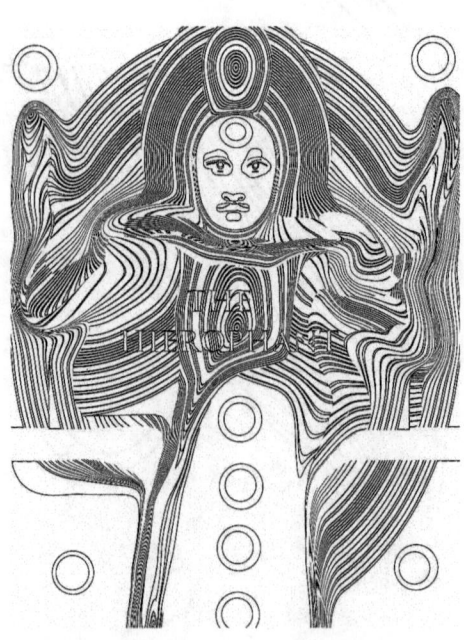

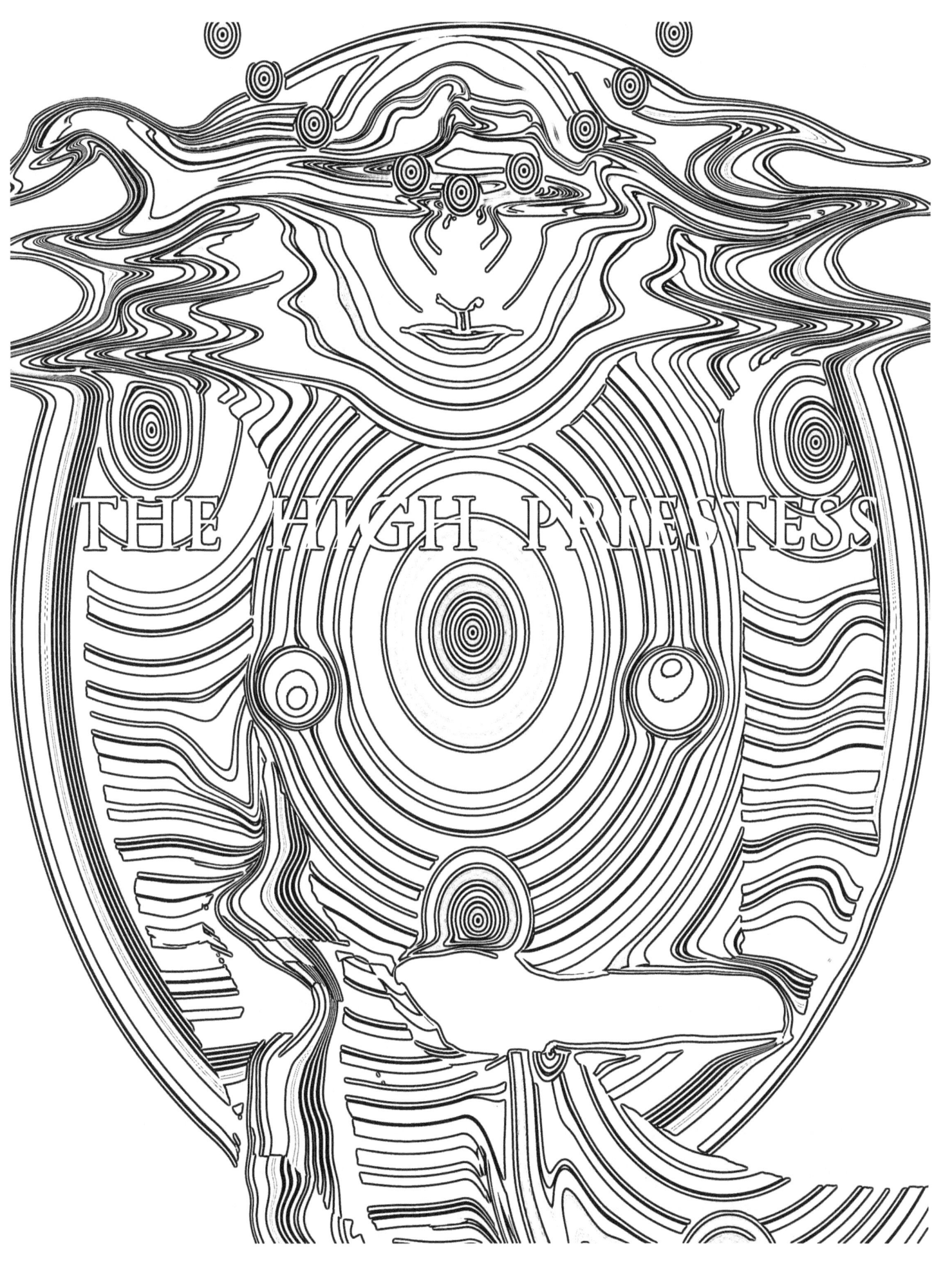

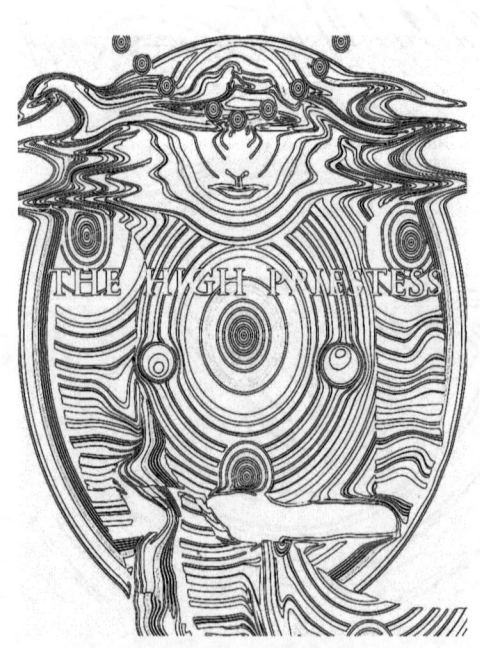
THE HIGH PRIESTESS

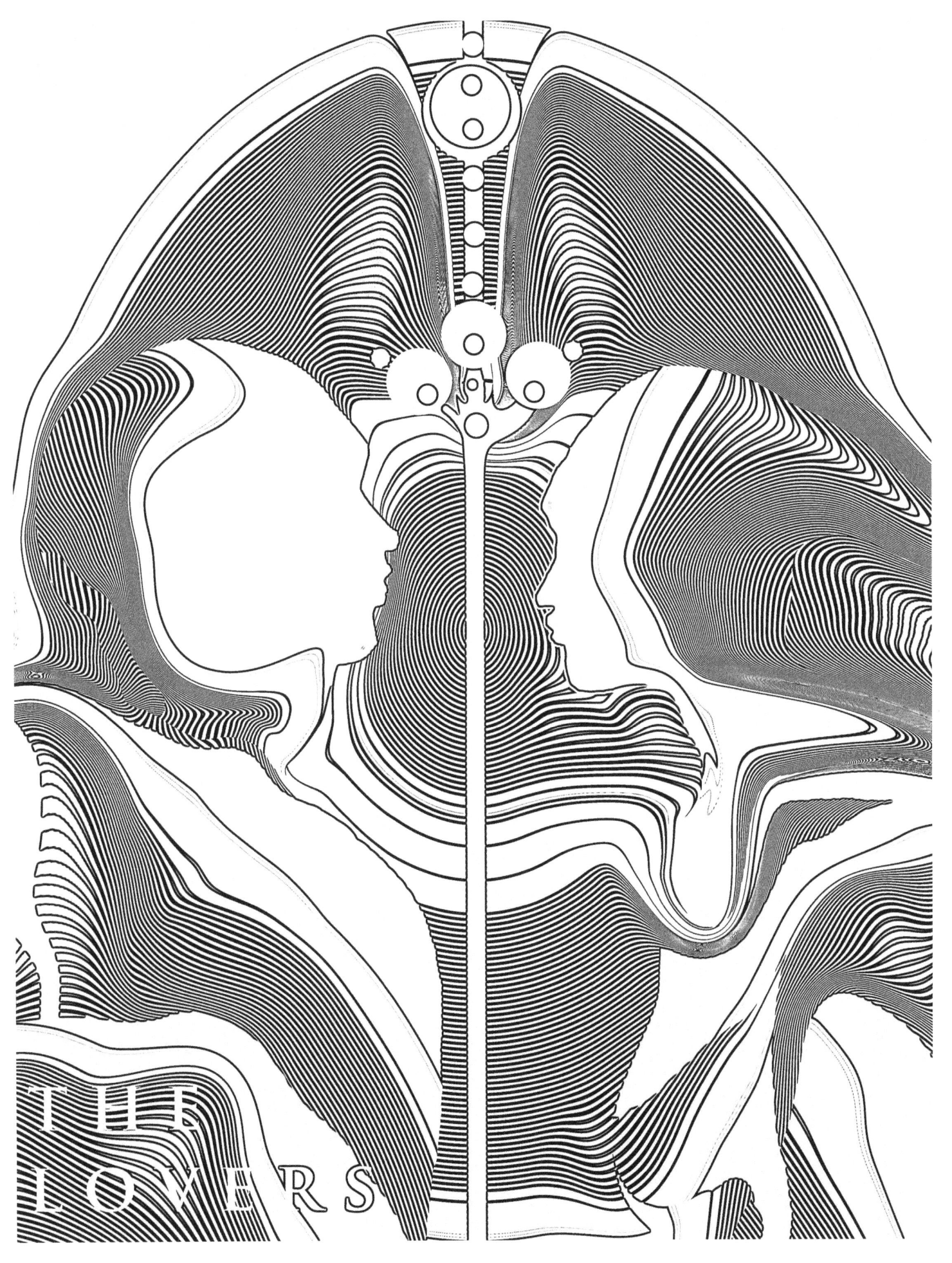

THE
LOVERS

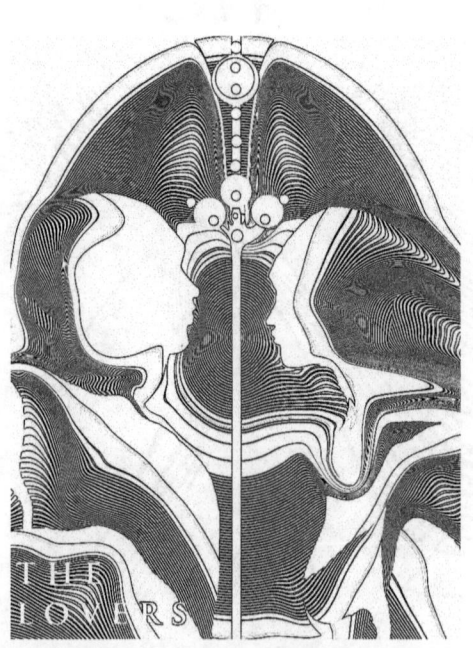

THE
LOVERS

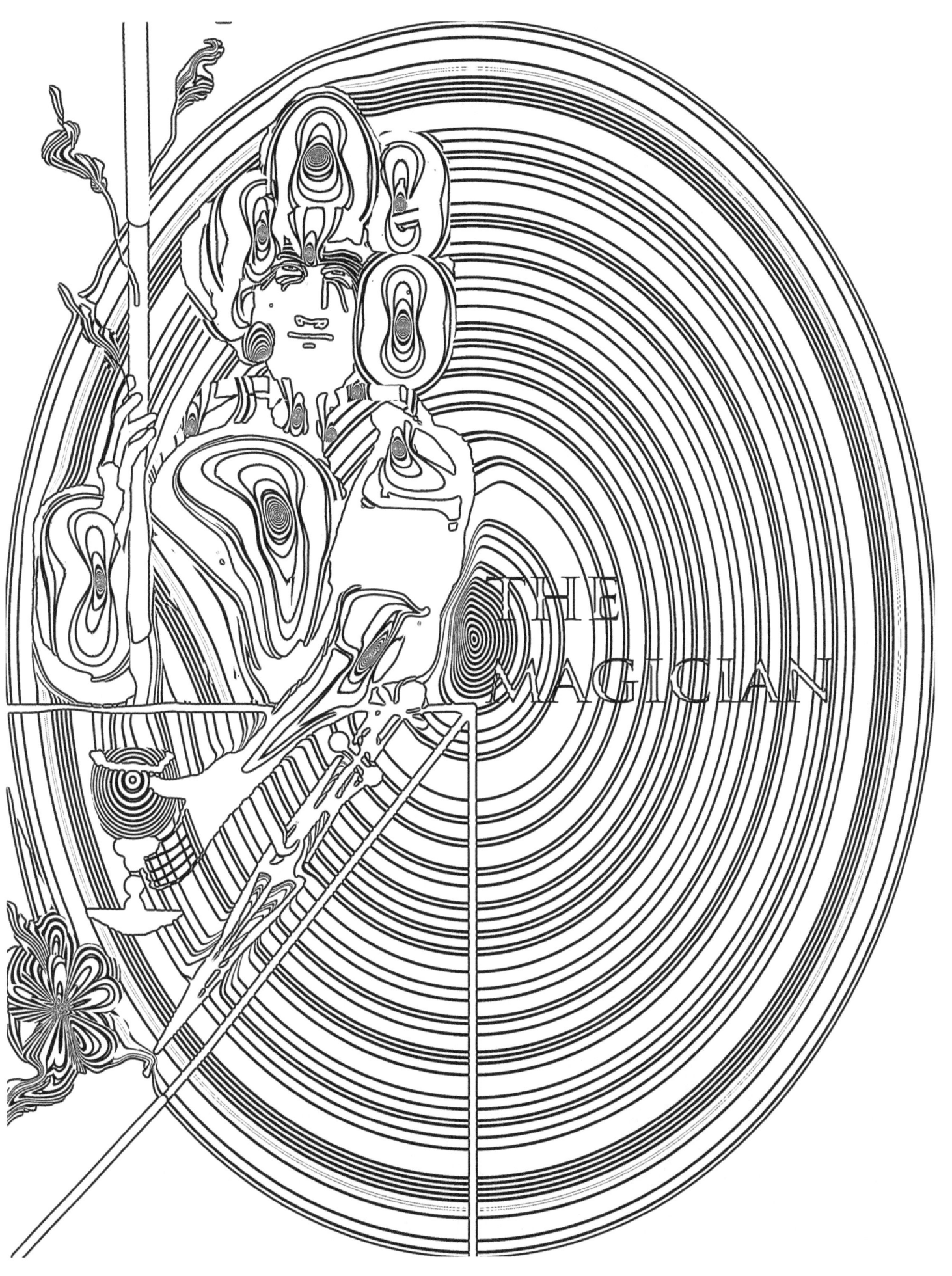

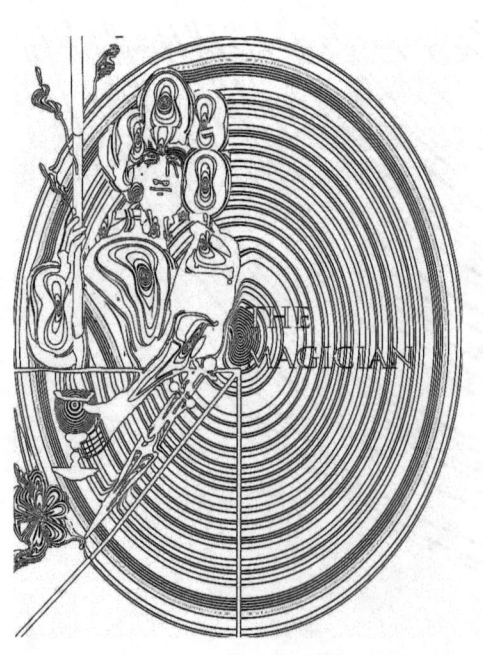

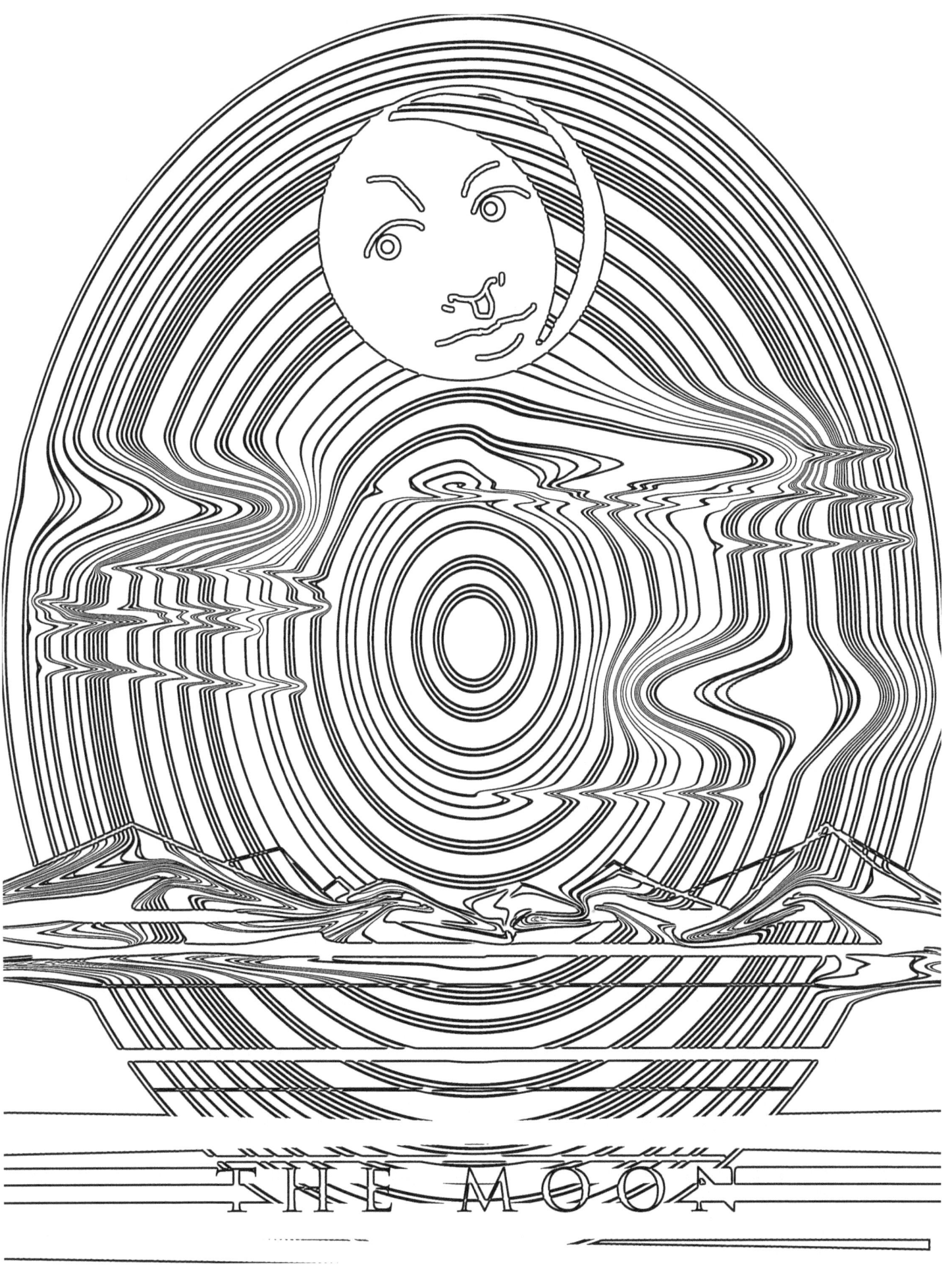

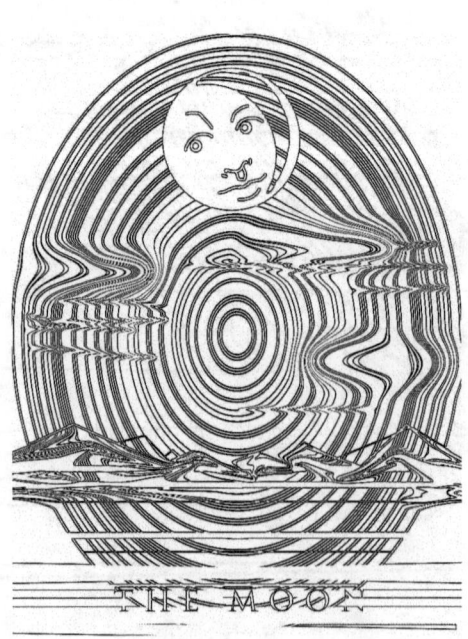

THE MOON

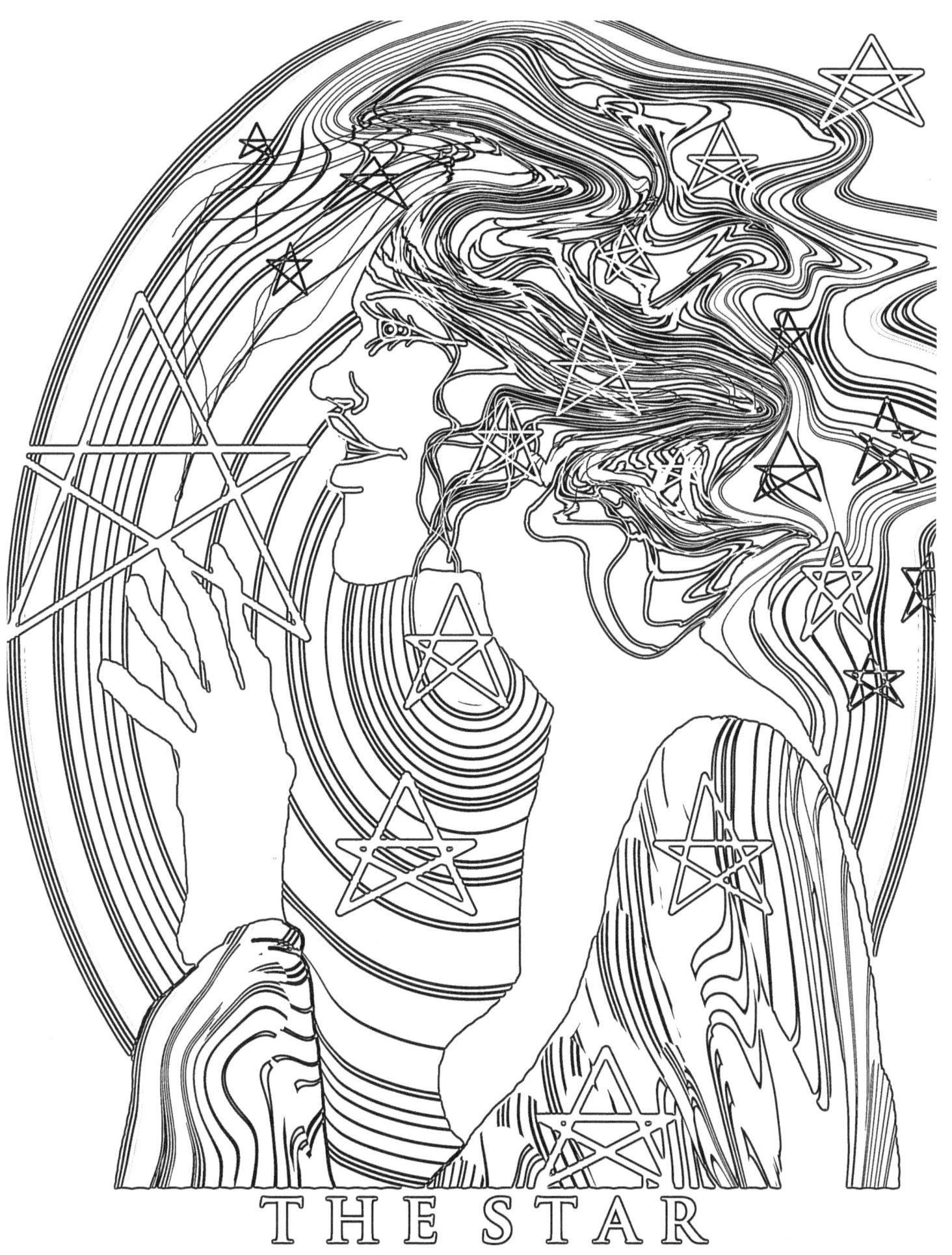

THE STAR

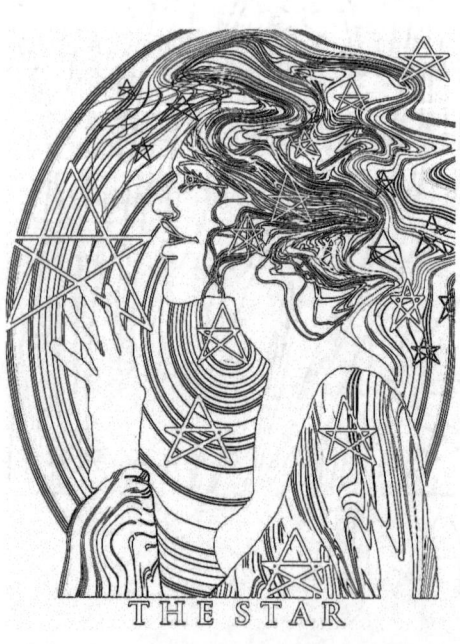

THE STAR

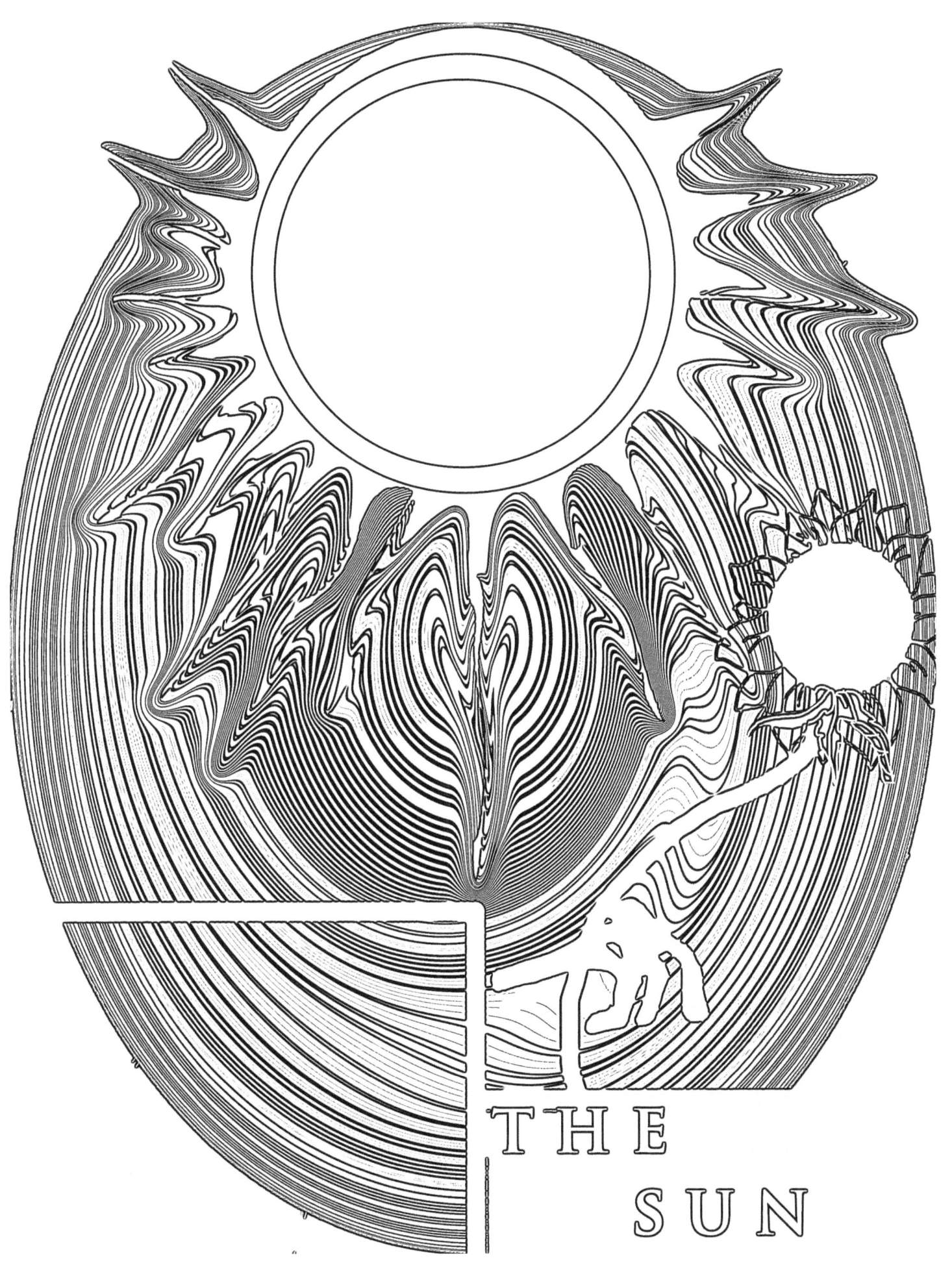

THE

SUN

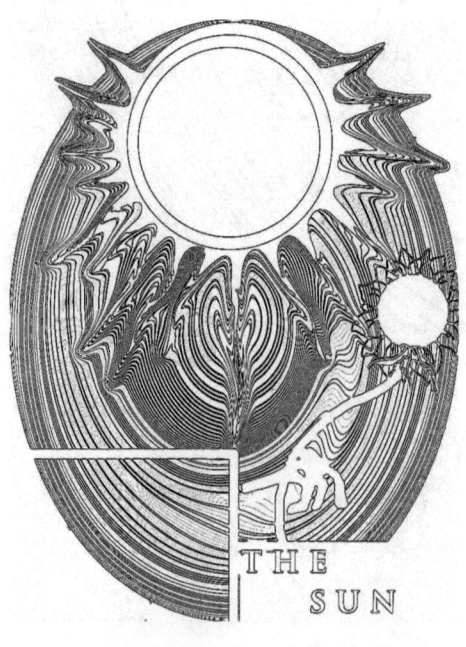

THE SUN

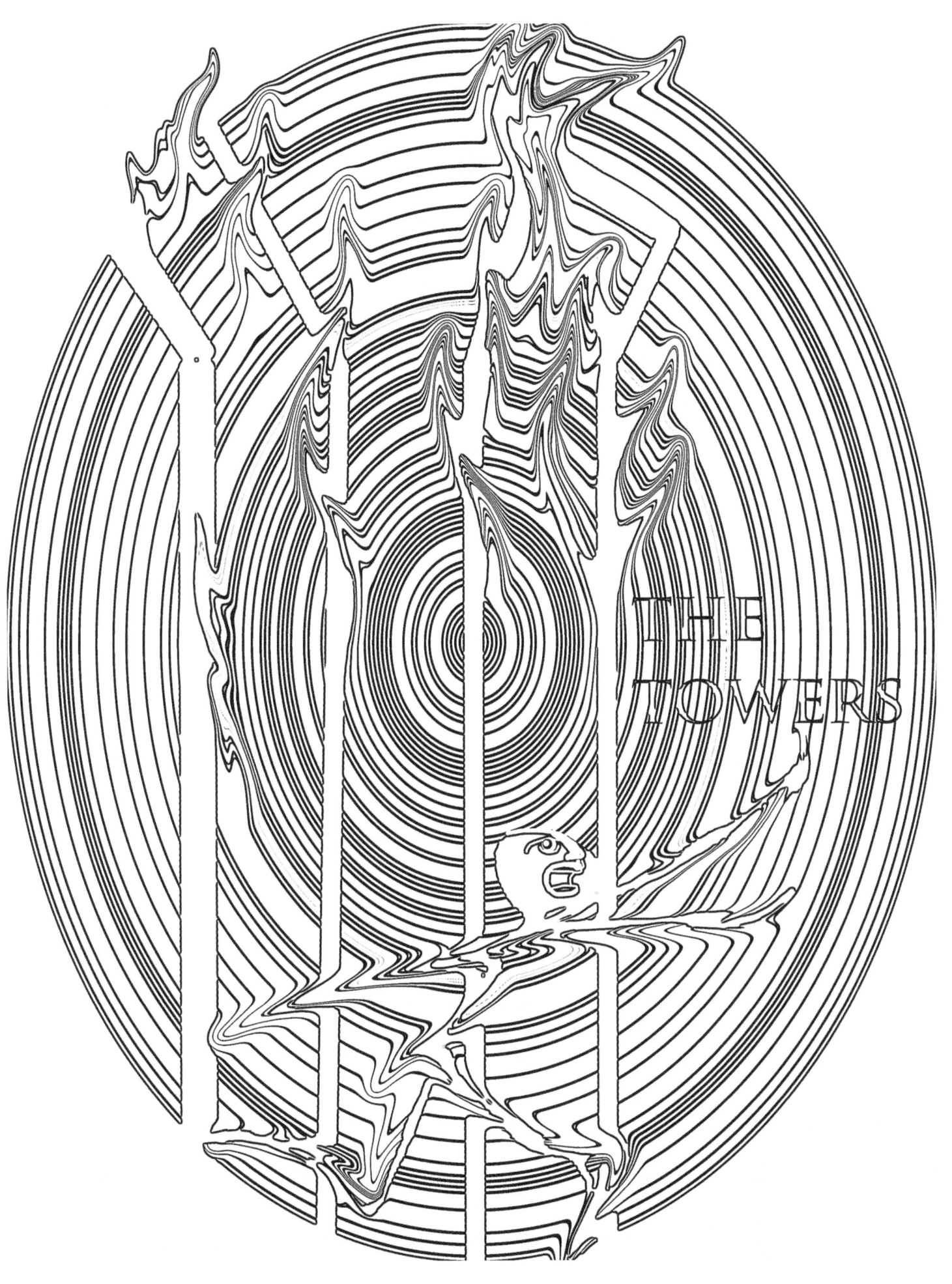

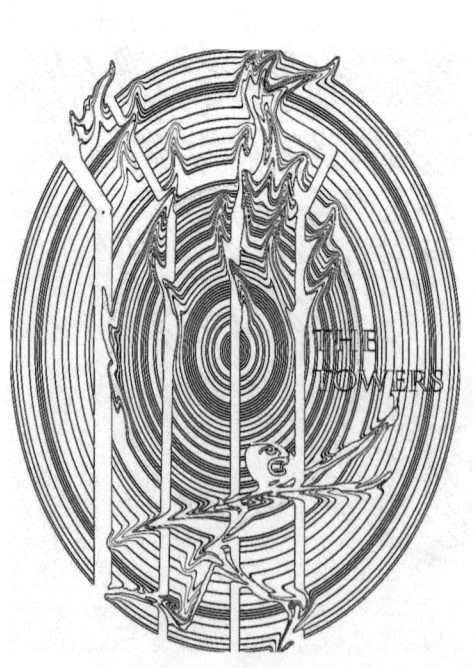

THE
TOWERS

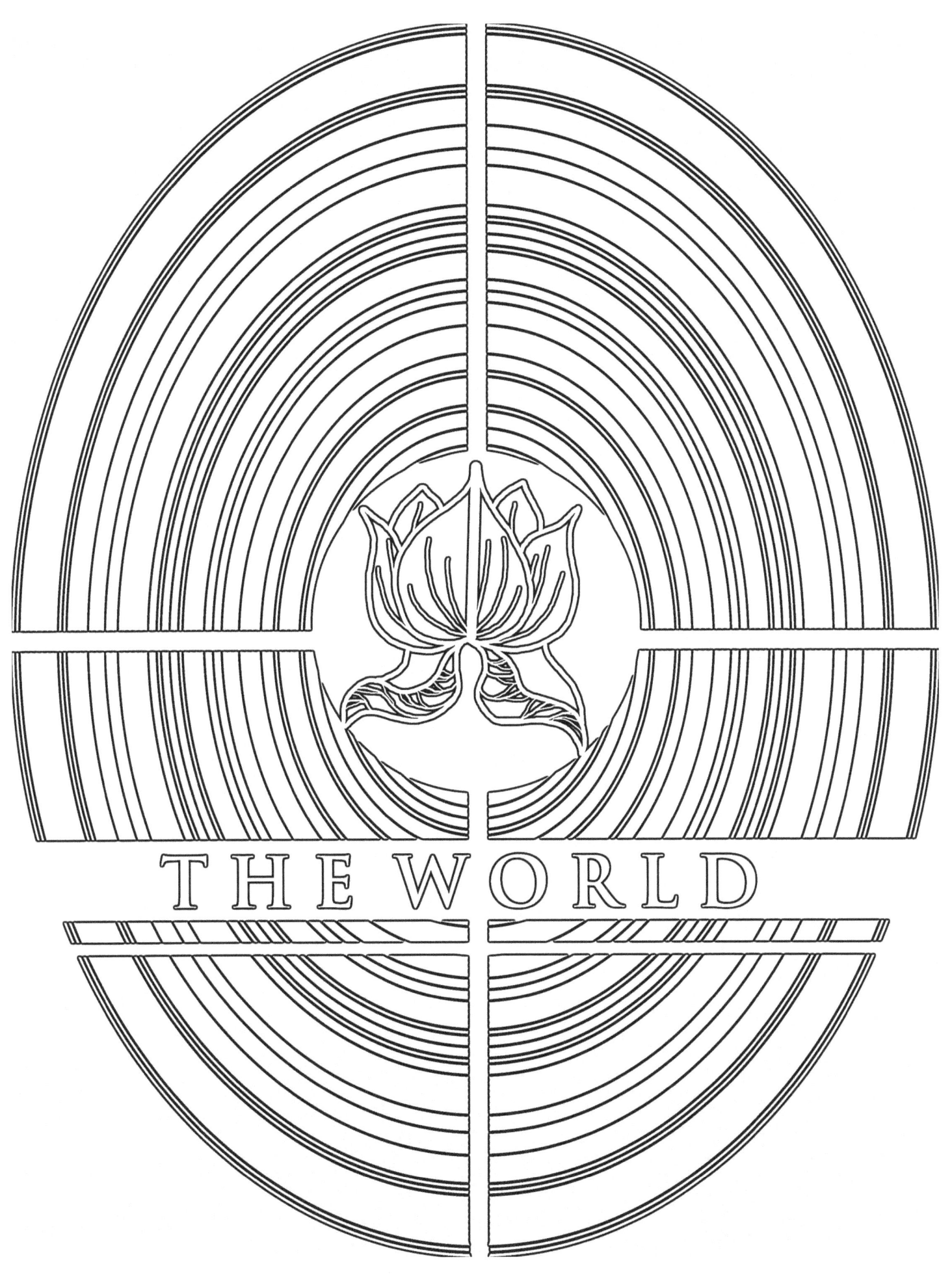

THE WORLD

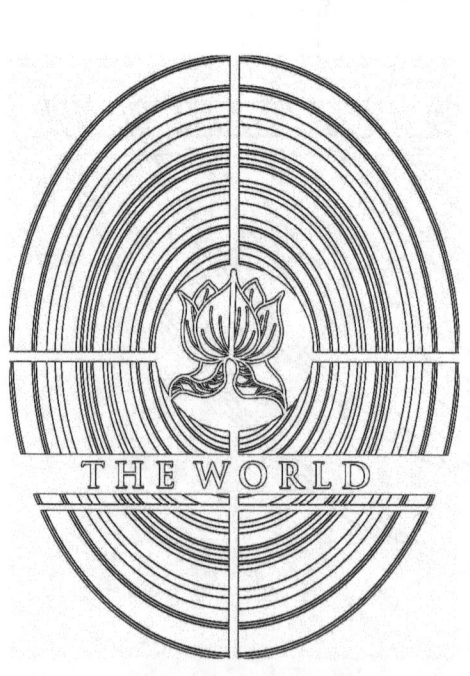
THE WORLD

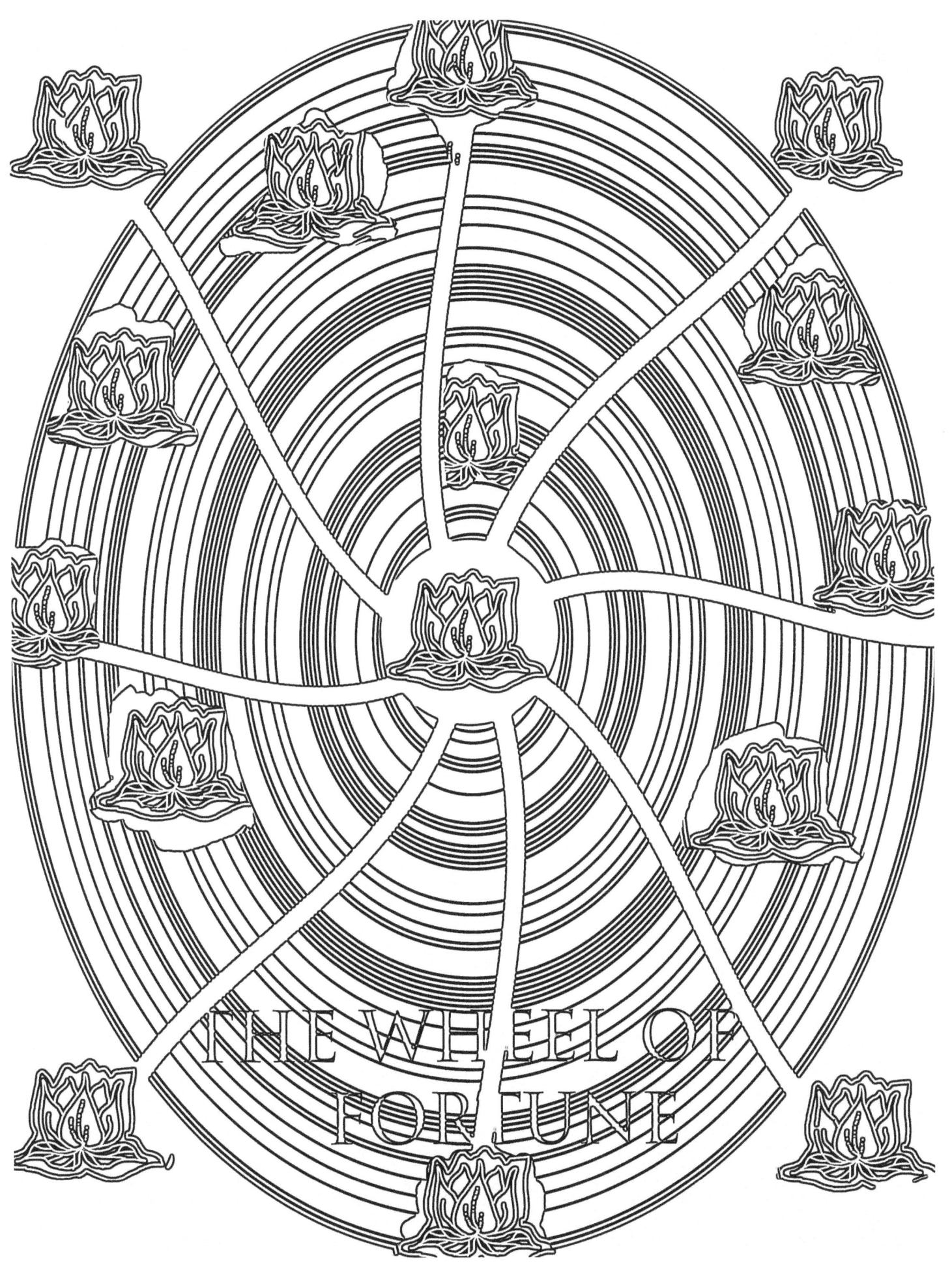

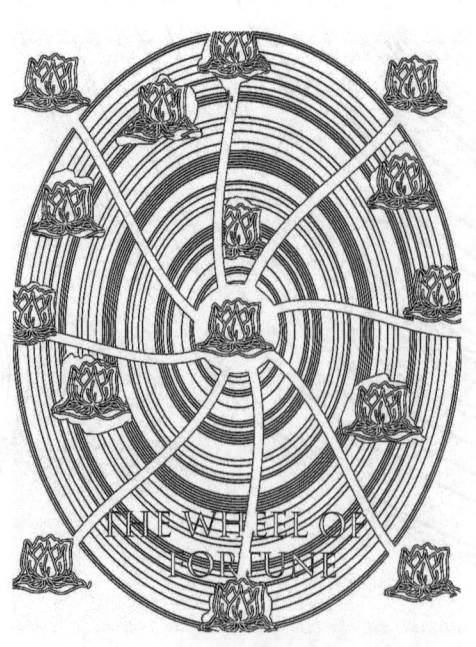

THE WHEEL OF
FORTUNE

Also in this Series…

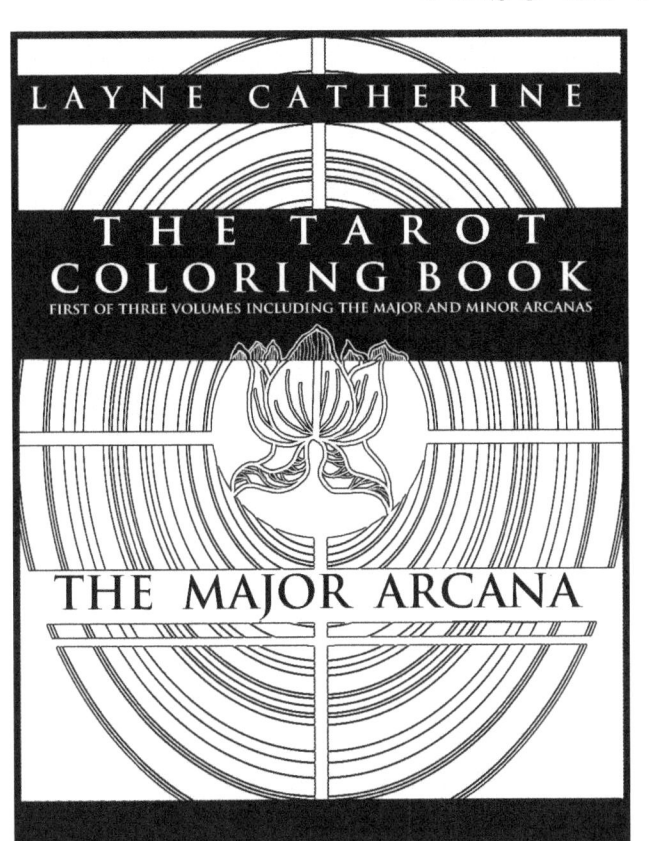

THIS BOOK

THE MAJOR ARCANA

BOOK No.1 IN THIS SERIES

THE MINOR ARCANAS

THE NEXT BOOK

THE LAST BOOK

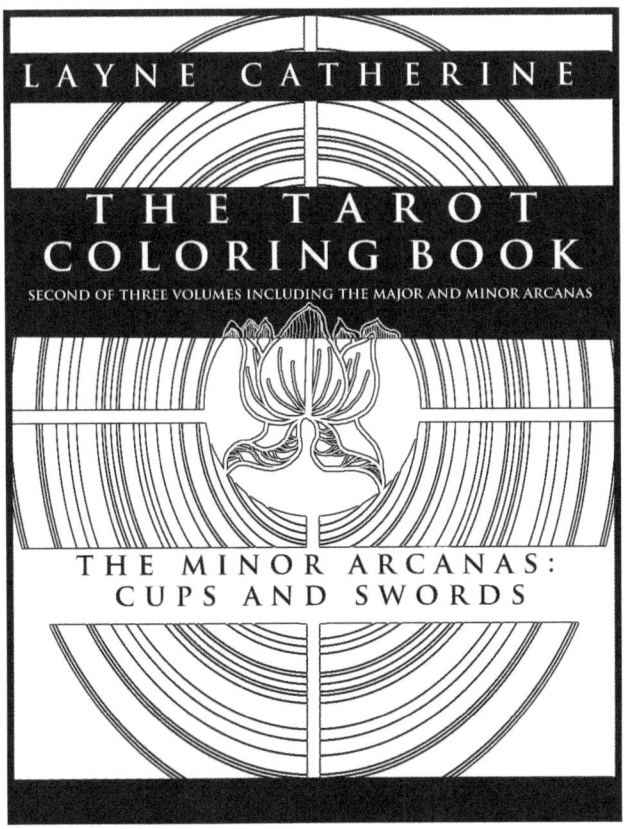

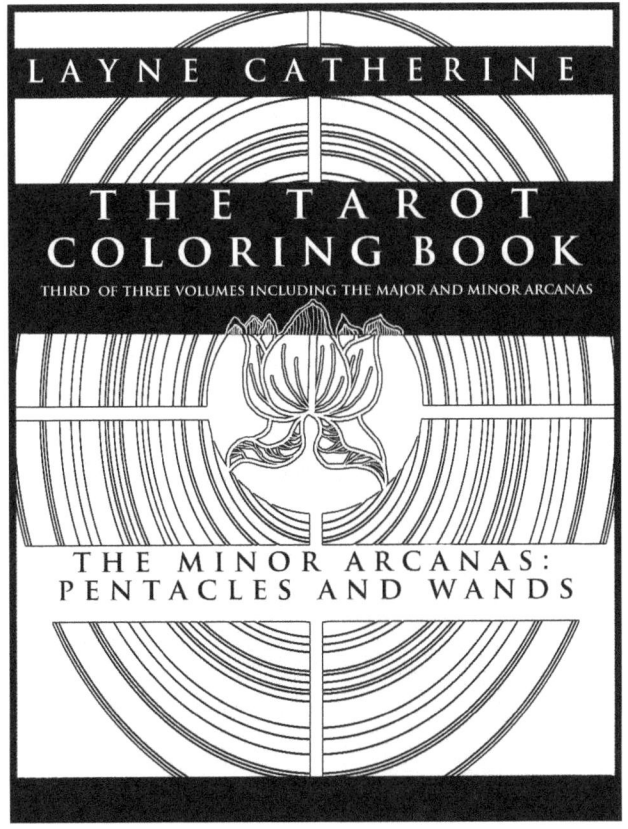

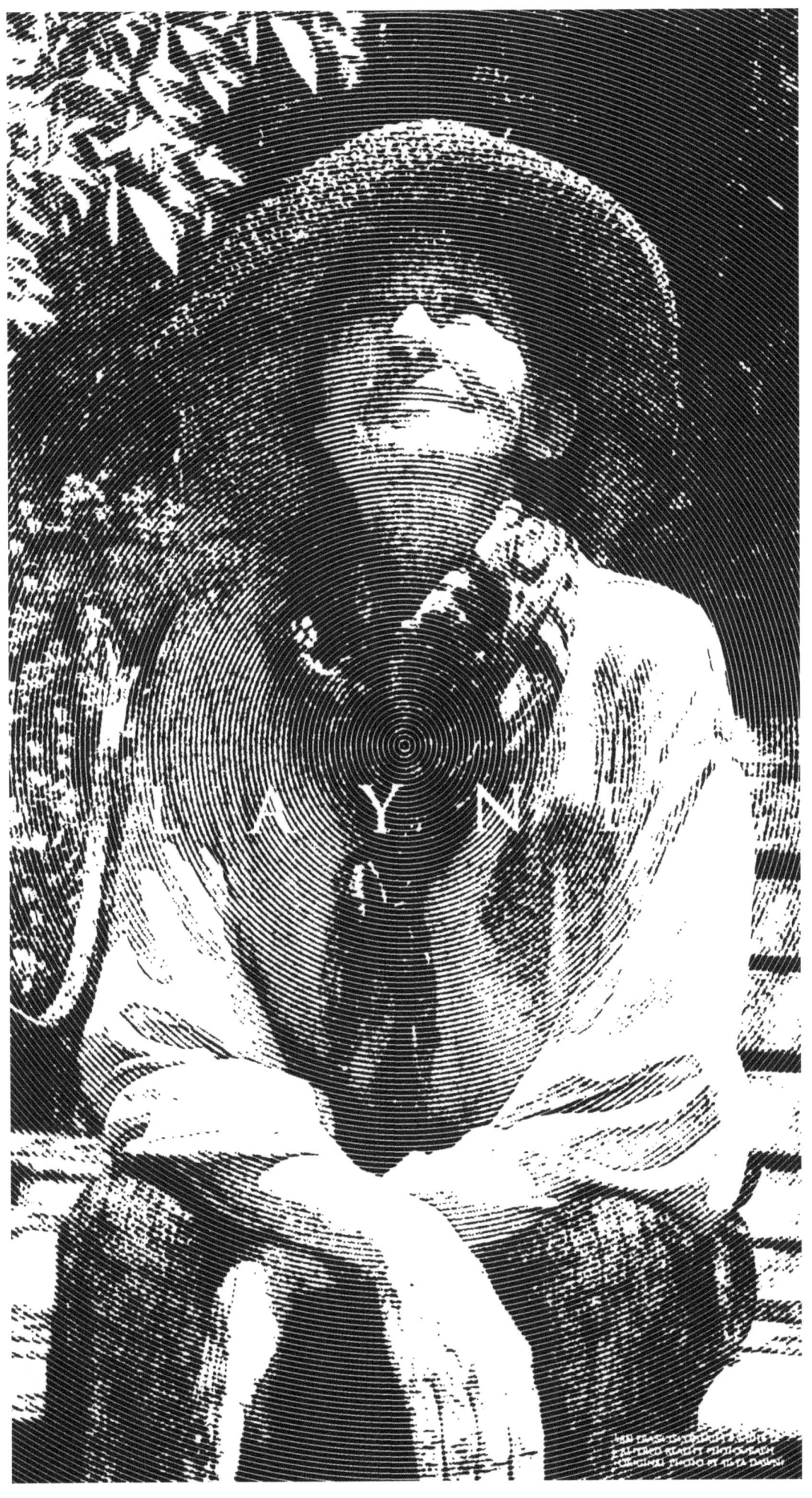

THE NEXT LAYNE CATHERINE COLORING BOOKS

MEDICINAL MARBLES

AND

TAO GEISHA

WILL BE AVAILABLE VERY SOON

AS WELL AS

MANDALAS, ELLIPSES, OPTICALS AND FANTASTIQUE IMAGERY SERIES

AND LOOK FOR A NEW SERIES OF MEDITATIONS ON

THE TWENTY FIRST CENTURY WOMAN

YOU WILL BE DELIGHTED TO ADD THESE TO YOUR GROWING COLLECTION OF LAYNE CATHERINE COLORING BOOKS

"YOU DO NOT HAVE TO STAY INSIDE THE LINES."

USE THIS PAGE TO TEST YOUR COLORING MATERIALS AND PUT A PLAIN PIECE OF PAPER UNDER THE PAGE THAT YOU ARE COLORING FOR THE BEST RESULTS.